"With a goal of generating hope for Chr[...] pluralistic world, Volf encourages Christians to share and receive gifts of spiritual wisdom, to speak truth in their distinct religious voice, and to live generously with people of other faiths. This insightful exploration of how Christians may faithfully engage today's political and pluralistic culture provides accessible, wise guidance for people of all faiths."

—*Publishers Weekly* (starred review)

"At once erudite and accessible, Volf explores the place and role of religion, Christianity in particular, in public life. . . . He wrestles with many of the most vexing contemporary questions, such as the alleged link between faith and violence."

—**Anthony B. Robinson**, *Christian Century*

"Volf puts his finger on one of the most relevant and hotly contested subjects in our world today—the role of faith in public life. . . . When people start taking their faith commitments and living them publicly in a pluralistic world they are bound to encounter others who, equally convicted, are living out their faith. This is at the root of so much violence in our world. For Christians however, Volf is adamant that our role is not accommodation to the culture (idle faith) or the total transformation of the culture (coercive faith), but creative engagement with the world. . . . This book will be an invaluable resource to Christian communities who are working out for themselves what this creative engagement with the world looks like in their context."

—**Ryan J. Bell**, *Huffington Post*

"[Volf] is one of the best theological interpreters of America's current social, religious, and political landscape. . . . He's that rare breed of scholar-writer who can popularize erudite theology without diminishing its scope or masking its subtleties. . . . *A Public Faith* will make for interesting reading. . . . As candidates and their partisan backers exploit religious language for political gain, Volf has provided the conceptual and linguistic tools for changing the terms of a tired debate."

—**Debra Dean Murphy**, *Englewood Review of Books*

"Volf offers an important argument for how difference and disagreement in public, including those of an 'engaged faith,' can be productive for our democratic politics."

—**Kenneth Sheppard**, *Patrol*

"This accessible political theology should be viewed as a significant revision of Richard Mouw's *Pluralisms and Horizons*. Moreover, it is not inconsequential that Volf constructs much of his proposal employing David Ford's compelling model of *Scriptural Reasoning* and Nicholas Wolterstorff's Christian philosophy, which wholeheartedly subscribes to a political pluralism. Read behind this whole text, once again, is Volf's personal history and struggle against the political coerciveness of communist Yugoslavia and the genocide that took place between Christians and Muslims from Serbia, Bosnia, and his native Croatia. A worthy read!"

—**Stuart Weir**, *Themelios*

"In any election year, debates rage about the role of religion in public life. This excellent volume should be required reading for all candidates running for public office, among others. . . . Excellent notes and index. . . . Recommended. Lower-division undergraduates through researchers/faculty; general readers."

—**G. H. Shriver**, *Choice*

"This is quite simply the right book at the right time by a well-respected Yale theologian who draws on some of the best writers among . . . mainline Protestant, evangelical, Catholic, and Orthodox thinkers, helping us navigate the complex cultural setting of pluralism, resentments about fundamentalisms, theological violence, and—still, at least until people read this book—a quietism that suggests we needn't think much about pubic life. . . . This is serious, nuanced, [and] evangelical in the best sense. . . . Give this to anybody you know who is active in activism or public discourse."

—**Byron Borger**, heartsandmindsbooks.com

"Volf's irenic expression of the role of Christian faith in public life is a breath of fresh air in the midst of the foul winds of today's culture wars. . . . Volf's book is thought-provoking and insightful. In defending his case for an 'engaged faith,' he carefully probes the models available to us and steers a middle path between secularism and theocracy. Both of these extreme sides in today's culture will benefit from reading this fine little book."

—**Kurt Peterson**, *Covenant Companion*

A PUBLIC
FAITH

How Followers of Christ
Should Serve the Common Good

MIROSLAV VOLF

BrazosPress
a division of Baker Publishing Group
Grand Rapids, Michigan

Published by Brazos Press
a division of Baker Publishing Group
P.O. Box 6287, Grand Rapids, MI 49516-6287
www.brazospress.com

Printed in the United States of America

Paperback edition published 2013
ISBN 978-1-58743-343-6

The Library of Congress has cataloged the hardcover edition as follows:
Volf, Miroslav.
       A public faith : how followers of Christ should serve the common good /
  Miroslav Volf.
          p.   cm.
       Includes bibliographical references (p.   ) and index.
       ISBN 978-1-58743-298-9 (cloth)
       1. Christian sociology. 2. Common good—Religious aspects—Christianity.
  I. Title.
  BT738.V66 2011
  261.7—dc22   2011010734

The internet addresses, email addresses, and phone numbers in this book are accurate at the time of publication. They are provided as a resource. Baker Publishing Group does not endorse them or vouch for their content or permanence.

16   17   18   19   20   21   22   9 8 7 6 5 4 3

In keeping with biblical principles of creation stewardship, Baker Publishing Group advocates the responsible use of our natural resources. As a member of the Green Press Initiative, our company uses recycled paper when possible. The text paper of this book is composed in part of post-consumer waste.

To Skip

Contents

Introduction

Debates are raging today about the role of religions in public life, and it is not difficult to see why. First, religions—Buddhism, Judaism, Christianity, Islam, and so on—are growing numerically, and their members worldwide are increasingly unwilling to keep their convictions and practices limited to the private sphere of family or religious community. Instead, they want these convictions and practices to shape public life. They may engage in electoral politics and seek to influence legislative processes (as the Religious Right has done in the United States since the Reagan presidency), or they may concentrate on transforming the moral fabric of society through religious awakening (as the Religious Right seems to be doing during the Obama presidency). Either way, many religious people aim to shape public life according to their own vision of the good life.

Second, in today's globalized world, religions cannot be neatly sequestered into separate geographic areas. As the world shrinks and the interdependence of people increases, ardent proponents of different religions come to inhabit the same space. But how do such people live together, especially when all of them want to shape the public realm according to the dictates of their own sacred texts and traditions?

When it comes to the public role of religions, the main fear is that of imposition—one faith imposing aspects of its own way of life on others. Religious people fear imposition—Muslims fear Christians, Christians fear Muslims, Jews fear both, Muslims fear Jews, Hindus fear Muslims, Christians fear Hindus, and so on. Secularists, those who subscribe to no traditional religious faith at all, fear imposition as well—imposition by any faith—since they tend to deem all of them irrational and dangerous.

The fear of imposition of religious views often elicits demands for the suppression of religious voices from the public square. The people espousing that view argue that politics, one major public sphere, should "remain unilluminated by the light of revelation" and should be guided by human reason alone, as Mark Lilla has put it recently.[1] This is the idea of a secular state, forged over the last few centuries in the West.

Religious Totalitarianism

Unlike those who think religion should stay out of politics, I will argue in this book that religious people ought to be free to bring their visions of the good life into the public sphere—into politics as well as other aspects of public life. What's more, I believe that it would be oppressive to prohibit them from doing so. But as soon as one starts making such an argument, some people raise the threat of religious totalitarianism.[2]

For many secularists today, militant Islam, represented by a figure like Sayyid Qutb, shows how religions, if allowed free reign, would behave in the public realm. This represents a massive misunderstanding of religions, but it is the ghost that haunts discussions of the public role of religion. To get this "ghost" clearly into view, I will sketch briefly Qutb's position as articulated in *Milestones*, a short and revolutionary book he wrote in prison (1954–64), which earned him a death sentence in 1966. Qutb has been described as "the godfather of radical Islam"; what Marx was to Communism, it is said, Qutb has been to radical Islam. This is an exaggeration. It is true, however, that he has been "the major influence on the worldview of radical movements across the Muslim world."[3] To me, he is the most compelling and presently most influential representative of what I would describe as religious totalitarianism—more intellectually rigorous than contemporary Christian representatives of religious totalitarianism, such as the so called "dominion theologians."[4] The position that I myself will advocate in this book will be an alternative both to the secular total exclusion of all religions from public life and to Qutb's total saturation of public life with a single religion.

I am a Christian and Qutb is a Muslim. But the contrast I am drawing is *not* between Christian and Islamic positions. For a great majority of Muslims, Qutb's position is completely unacceptable, faithful neither to the authoritative sources of Islam nor to the centuries-long experience of Muslims with a variety of political arrangements in many parts of the world. The contrast is rather between religious political pluralism and religious totalitarianism. The position I designate here as "religious political pluralism" emerged within Christianity, but it is not *the* Christian position. Not all Christians embrace it, and some in the last few centuries have strenuously objected to it. Inversely, among people of faith, it is not Christians alone who today embrace religious political pluralism. Many Jews, Buddhists, and Muslims, among others, embrace it as well.[5]

Here is the bare-bones sketch of Qutb's argument:

1. Since there is "no god but God"—*the* basic Muslim conviction—God has absolute sovereignty on earth. For

traditional Jews and Christians no less than for Muslims, this is an uncontested claim. But many followers of Abrahamic religions consider the implications Qutb draws from it deeply problematic.

2. That God alone is God means for Qutb that all authority of human beings—whether priests, politicians, or ordinary people—over others is illicit. *Every* human authority (except that of prophet Muhammad as the mouthpiece of God) is an idol, and compromises God's oneness and sovereignty.

3. Guidance as to how to lead one's personal life and how to organize social life comes from God alone (as revealed through the prophet Muhammad). Just as the one God "does not forgive any association [of another divinity] with His person," so God does "not accept any association with His revealed way of life."[6] Obeying the commands from some other source than God is as much idolatry as is worshiping another deity.

4. Islam is not a set of beliefs, but a way of life in total submission to the rule of the one God. The Muslim community is "the name of a group of people whose manners, ideas and concepts, rules and regulations, values and criteria, are all derived from the Islamic source."[7]

Qutb sums up the internal constitution of the Muslim community in the following way: "No god but God" means "no sovereignty except God's, no law except from God, and no authority of one man over another, as the authority in all respects belongs to God."[8] A community that embraces these principles as a way of life is a Muslim community. It is exclusive and its rules regulate all aspects of its members' lives. This is its internal constitution. What about its external relations?

1. Muslims are called to cut themselves off completely from communities that exhibit ignorance of the guidance of God.

2. Since God is one and the Creator, the law of God that regulates human personal and social life, as formulated by the prophet Muhammad, is no less universal than the so-called laws of nature; both laws apply always and everywhere.

3. "The foremost duty of Islam in this world is to depose *Jahiliyyah* [ignorance of the divine guidance] from the leadership of man, and to take the leadership into its own hands and enforce the particular way of life which is its permanent feature."[9]

4. Muslims are called to embrace the faith that there is "no god but God"—a faith that must be embraced freely, since there is no compulsion in religion.

Imposition of the rule of one God, as interpreted by the prophet Muhammad, on the whole world—this is the mission of political Islam as interpreted by Qutb. There can be religious freedom properly understood only within a political order that embodies the Muslim way of life. Political Islam is religious at its basis, and, unlike the mainstream of Islam, it is aggressively totalitarian in its character.[10] "There is only one place on earth which can be called the home of Islam (Dar-ul-Islam)," he writes in summary of his position,

> and it is that place where the Islamic state is established and Shariah is the authority and God's limits are observed and where all the Muslims administer the affairs of the state with mutual consultation. The rest of the world is the home of hostility (Dar-ul-Harb).[11]

A reminder one more time: this is not *the* Islamic position. The great majority of Muslims—including the most influential religious and secular scholars—disagree with it. This is an *extremist version* of the Islamic position, whose author is not a trained Islamic scholar. For me here, it functions as an example of the kind of religious totalitarianism that members of various faiths, including Christianity, have advocated in the past and still continue to advocate today.[12]

Toward an Alternative

In this small volume I offer a sketch of an alternative to totalitarian saturation of public life with a single religion as well as to secular exclusion of all religions from public life. I am writing as a Christian theologian to followers of Christ. I am not writing as a generic religious person to adherents of all religions, a project that would fail from the start. To stay with the example of Qutb, it is a task of Muslim scholars to elaborate distinctly Islamic alternatives to Qutb. My task is to offer a vision of the role of the followers of Jesus Christ in public life, a role that stays clear of the dangers of both "exclusion" and "saturation."

One of the most widely discussed Christian texts about the relation between religion and culture, including politics, is H. Richard Niebuhr's *Christ and Culture*.[13] Writing in the mid-1950s, he analyzed five Christian stances toward culture: Christ against Culture, the Christ of Culture, Christ above Culture, Christ and Culture in Paradox, and Christ Transforming Culture. If we used Niebuhr's categories, we could say that Qutb's position is a combination of sectarian "religion against culture" and politically activist "religion transforming culture" with the goal of achieving identity between religion and culture.

As Niebuhr's typology suggests, in the Christian tradition— and something similar is true of other religions—there is more than one way to relate religion to culture. And even Niebuhr's various types are broad and abstract, as is appropriate for the ideal types he intends them to be. The actual representatives of these five stances toward culture are less clear-cut and tend to combine elements from more than one category.

My contention in this book is that there is no single way in which Christian faith relates and ought to relate to culture as a whole (see chapter 5). The relation between faith and culture is too complex for that. Faith stands in opposition to some elements of culture and is detached from others. In some aspects faith is identical with elements of culture, and it seeks to transform in diverse ways yet many more. Moreover, faith's stance toward culture changes over time as culture changes. How, then, is the stance of faith toward culture defined? It is—or it ought to be—defined by the center of the faith itself, by its relation to Christ as the divine Word incarnate and the Lamb of God who takes away the sin of the world.

The center of the Christian faith suggests a relation to the broader culture that can be roughly described in the following six points:

1. Christ is God's Word and God's Lamb, come into the world for the good of all people, who are all God's creatures and loved by God. Christian faith is therefore a "prophetic" faith that seeks to mend the world. An idle or redundant faith—a faith that does not seek to mend the world—is a seriously malfunctioning faith (see chapters 1 and 2). Faith should be active in all spheres of life: education and arts, business and politics, communication and entertainment, and more.

2. Christ came to redeem the world by preaching, actively helping people, and dying a criminal's death on behalf of the ungodly. In all aspects of his work, he was a bringer of grace. A coercive faith—a faith that seeks to impose itself and its way of life on others through any form of

coercion—is also a seriously malfunctioning faith (see chapters 1 and 3).

3. When it comes to life in the world, to follow Christ means to care for others (as well as for oneself) and work toward their flourishing, so that life would go well for all and so that all would learn how to lead their lives well (see chapter 4). A vision of human flourishing and the common good is the main thing the Christian faith brings into the public debate.

4. Since the world is God's creation and since the Word came to his own even if his own did not accept him (John 1:11), the proper stance of Christians toward the larger culture cannot be that of unmitigated opposition or whole-scale transformation. A much more complex attitude is required—that of accepting, rejecting, learning from, transforming, and subverting or putting to better uses various elements of an internally differentiated and rapidly changing culture (see chapter 5).

5. Jesus Christ is described in the New Testament as a "faithful witness" (Rev. 1:5) and his followers understood themselves as witnesses (e.g., Acts 5:32). The way Christians work toward human flourishing is not by imposing on others their vision of human flourishing and the common good but by bearing witness to Christ, who embodies the good life (see chapter 6).

6. Christ has not come with a blueprint for political arrangements; many kinds of political arrangements are compatible with the Christian faith, from monarchy to democracy. But in a pluralistic context, Christ's command "in everything do to others as you would have them do to you" (Matt. 7:12) entails that Christians grant to other religious communities the same religious and political freedoms that they claim for themselves. Put differently,

Christians, even those who in their own religious views are exclusivists, ought to embrace pluralism as a political project (see chapter 7).[14]

This is, in broad strokes, the alternative that I propose to religious totalitarianism, and it sums up the main content of the book.

I explore three simple questions in the following pages:

1. In what ways does the Christian faith malfunction in the contemporary world, and how should we counter these malfunctions (chapters 1–3)?
2. What should be the main concern of Christ's followers when it comes to living well in the world today (chapter 4)?
3. How should Christ's followers go about realizing their vision of living well in today's world in relation to other faiths and together with diverse people with whom they live under the roof of a single state (chapters 5–7)?

In trying to answer these simple questions, my goal is to offer an alternative both to secular exclusion of religion from the public sphere and to all forms of "religious totalitarianism"—an alternative predicated not on attenuating Christian convictions but on affirming them robustly and living them out joyously.

PART I

COUNTERING
FAITH'S
MALFUNCTIONS

1

Malfunctions of Faith

When I introduce the Yale Center for Faith and Culture, which I direct, to an audience for the first time, I often show the seal of the Center, depicting an open book with a white page and a green leaf. I ask the audience what they see.

"New life springing out of a book?" someone may suggest.

"The book is the book of learning," another person might offer.

"No, it's the Word of God," somebody else may explain, to bring the symbol closer to the substance of faith.

"Why not both?" another will chime in while pointing out that symbols may have multiple meanings and that the Center's name includes both faith and culture.

"And what about the green leaf?" I inquire.

"It stands for a thriving culture growing out of the Scriptures, out of faith," says someone else, trying to connect all the dots.

"Yes," I respond, and continue, "the image of the leaf was inspired by the tree mentioned at the end of the book of Revelation, whose leaves are for the 'healing of the nations.'" That's what we at the Center are all about—promoting the practice of Christian faith in all spheres of life so that what is broken in our individual lives and cultures can be mended, and we all can flourish as God's creatures—finite, fragile, flawed, and in all this glorious. More important, that's also what the Christian faith as a prophetic religion is about.

Malfunctions

In the course of Christianity's long history—full of remarkable achievements by its saints and thinkers, artists and builders, reformers and ordinary folks—the Christian faith has sometimes failed to live up to its own standards as a prophetic religion. Too often, it neither mends the world nor helps human beings thrive. To the contrary, it seems to shatter things into pieces, to choke up what is new and beautiful before it has a chance to take root, to trample underfoot what is good and true. When this happens, faith is no longer a spring of fresh water helping good life to grow lushly, but a poisoned well, more harmful to those who drink its waters than any single vice could possibly be—as Friedrich Nietzsche, a fierce critic of Christianity, put it in his last and angrily prophetic book, *The Anti-Christ*.[1]

True, some of faith's damaging effects can be attributed largely to differences of perspective. Nietzsche, for example, valued power highly and hence derided Christianity for its "active sympathy for the ill-constituted and weak."[2] But in the face-off between Nietzsche's power and Christ's pity, faith ends up deleterious only if you share the values of Nietzsche's anti-faith.

Or take a concrete issue such as abortion. If you think that an unborn life is human and therefore sacred, then a faith that puts a mother's choice above respect for unborn life will seem self-centered, oppressive, violent, and even murderous when human life is most vulnerable.[3] In contrast, if you think that an unborn life is not yet a human being, then a faith that seeks to protect that life while sacrificing the well-being of its mother and against her choices will seem disrespectful, oppressive, and sometimes even violent toward the mother.[4]

Not all of Christianity's failures are merely a matter of perspective, however. As we reflect on how followers of Christ can serve the common good, it is important to keep these ill effects in mind. I call them "malfunctions." In this chapter and the following two, I will explore some of these malfunctions of Christian faith. I won't address the concerns of those who believe that religion itself, and the Christian faith specifically, is just one massive malfunction of the human spirit and culture—people who draw their lineage from the great continental critics of religion such as Ludwig Feuerbach, Karl Marx, Friedrich Nietzsche, or Sigmund Freud. For them, there are no heavens through which to ascend and no God to encounter; there is only the world, this immeasurably vast and cold universe. Moreover, what's worse than believing that there is an Ultimate One when in fact there is no such One, is insisting with unshakeable stubbornness, born of the belief in the absolute, on shaping the world according to the precepts of a nonexistent God. From the perspective of such critics, religion appears as the very pinnacle of oppressive irrationality. But I won't deal here with religion as a malfunction; I'll deal with malfunctions of religion, and of the Christian faith in particular.

In part 2 of the book I will argue that in order to counter malfunctions of faith, it is important for Christians to keep focused on God and on the proper understanding of human flourishing. For this, in the end, is what the Christian faith as a prophetic religion is all about—being an instrument of God for the sake of human flourishing, in this life and the next.

Prophetic Religions

In order to understand the Christian faith's malfunctions properly, it may be helpful to recall the old distinction between prophetic and mystical types of religion. The first advocates active transformation of the world, and the second encourages flights of the soul to God.[5]

Commenting on a widely held Muslim belief that from the place where the Dome of the Rock now stands in Jerusalem the prophet Muhammad ascended through the seven heavens to the very presence of God, a great Sufi mystic, Abdul Quddus of Gangoh, said, "Muhammad of Arabia ascended the highest Heaven and returned. I swear by God that if I had reached that point, I should never have returned." Quddus's statement reveals a basic difference between the prophetic and the mystical types of religion. In the words of Pakistani Muslim philosopher and statesman Muhammad Iqbal (d. 1938), from whose book *The Reconstruction of Religious Thought in Islam* I have taken the quote,

> The mystic does not wish to return from the repose of "unitary experience"; and even when he does return as he must, his return does not mean much for mankind at large. The prophet's return is creative. He returns to insert himself into the sweep of time with a view to control the forces of history, and thereby create a fresh world of ideals. . . . The desire to see his religious experience transformed into a living world-force is supreme in the prophet. Thus his return amounts to a kind of pragmatic test of the value of his religious experience.[6]

If we apply Iqbal's comment generally to prophetic religions rather than specifically to Muhammad, we may quibble with him about whether prophets ought to have the ambition to "control the forces of history," about the strict supremacy in the life of prophets of the desire to transform religious experience into "a living world-force," or about the "pragmatic test of the value of his religious experience." Nevertheless, Iqbal's basic point is compelling, and applicable beyond Islam: prophetic religions aim to transform the world in God's name rather than to flee from the world into God's arms as do mystical religions.

Like mainstream Islam and Judaism, Christianity is a prophetic type of religion. These three great Abrahamic faiths, as they are sometimes called, differ slightly about the substance of the prophetic vision and about the appropriate modalities of prophets' insertion into the world in order to realize that vision. They agree, however, that an authentic religious experience should be a world-shaping force. "Unitary experiences," even when highly prized, are not an end in themselves; their purpose is at least in part the prophet's sending into the world. "Ascents," though essential, must be followed by "returns."

According to the Hebrew Scriptures, Moses ascended Mount Sinai and returned with the tables of the law (Exod. 24:12–13; 32:15–16). According to the hadith—authentic stories about the founder of Islam—Muhammad ascended to the very presence of God and returned to continue his world-altering mission. A similar pattern applies, in a qualified sense, to Jesus Christ, who for Christians is not only a prophet but the Word made flesh (John 1:14): he ascended the Mount of Transfiguration and returned to mend a world plagued by evil (Matt. 17:1–9; Mark 9:2–9; Luke 9:28–37); more fundamentally, Jesus came "from above" to bring healing and redemption (John 8:23) and, having ascended into heaven at the end of his earthly sojourn, will return once more to judge and transform the world (e.g., Matt. 25:31–46; 1 Thess. 4:15–17; Rev. 21:1–8).

The Christian faith malfunctions when it is practiced as a mystical religion in which ascent is followed by a *barren* rather than creative return, a return that has no positive purpose for the world but is merely an inevitable result of the inability of a flesh-and-blood human being to sustain unitive experience over time. But mystical malfunctions of faith are not a problem today. Though mystical faiths continue to exist, even some traditionally mystical faiths are acquiring a prophetic dimension, as the example of "engaged Buddhism" shows.[7] As to the Christian faith, its mystical malfunction is rare these days and is relatively inconsequential. We can leave it aside without risking much harm and concentrate on other more momentous malfunctions.

Ascent and Return

As the examples of Moses, Jesus, and Muhammad illustrate, for prophetic religions, both "ascent" and "return" are crucial. "Ascent" is the point at which, in the encounter with the divine, representatives of prophetic religions receive the message and their core identity is forged—whether through mystical union with God, through prophetic inspiration, or through deepened understanding of sacred texts. The ascent is the *receptive* moment. "Return" is the point at which, in interchange with the world, the message is spoken, enacted, built into liturgies or institutions, or embodied in laws. The return is the *creative* moment.

I have described ascent as receptive and return as creative. The descriptions are appropriate in that they zero in on the main thrust of what happens in ascent and return. And yet "ascent" is not *merely* receptive. In receiving, the prophets themselves are transformed—they acquire new insight; their character is changed. So ascent is very much creative—a case of creative receptivity. Similarly, the "return" need not be merely creative—the prophets unilaterally shaping social realities. They themselves may be shaped in the process, return then being a case of receptive creativity.

Keeping in mind this more complex understanding of prophetic receptivity and creativity, we can say that without the "receptive ascent," there is no transforming message from God; without the "creative return," there is no engagement in the transformation of the world. Leave out either one, and you no longer have prophetic religion. Together, "ascent" and "return" form the pulsating heart of prophetic religion—showing that though "prophetic" and "mystical" are contrasting types of religion, religious experiences and engagement with the world are both essential components of the prophetic type of religion.

So far I have spoken mainly about the founding figures of the Abrahamic faiths and the general character of these faiths as prophetic religions; I have not mentioned ordinary believers and their leaders. And yet, they too are involved. For a religion to maintain its prophetic character, ordinary believers and their leaders must replicate in their own way both the "ascent" and the "return" of the great founding figures. Indeed, the abiding character of these faiths as prophetic religions will primarily depend on the ascents and returns of these ordinary people. The founding figures establish the proper function of a religion (defined internally and independently of whether outsiders see that religion as true and its proper function as salutary); ordinary believers and their leaders either carry on this function creatively through history or make a religion malfunction—and mostly they do both of these things at the same time.

As two moments of prophetic religion, "ascent" and "return" are also the points at which the prophetic religions most seriously malfunction. Correspondingly, one can identify two categories of malfunctions: "ascent malfunctions" and "return malfunctions."

Ascent Malfunctions

Ascent malfunctions result from a breakdown in the prophet's encounter with the divine and reception of the message. There are two such malfunctions.

Functional Reduction

The first ascent malfunction consists in *functional reduction* of faith. It happens when practitioners of prophetic religions lose faith in the significance of the encounter with God *as* God and employ religious language to promote perspectives and practices whose content and driving force do not come from or are not integrally related to the core of the faith. No ascent has happened; instead, a *pretense* of ascent and of speaking and acting in the name of God is employed to promote preset desirable ends. Such "prophets" exploit the authority for their audiences of a god who has lost all authority for the prophets themselves. They have reduced the living God to a function of the prophets' religious language.

In the majority of situations, functional reduction is not a case of bad faith; rarely are the representatives of prophetic religion cynically out to manipulate people by using religious symbols they believe to be vacuous. Something subtler is happening. Gradually the language about God is hollowed out from within, maybe by lack of trust and inconsequential use, until only a shell remains. And then that shell is put to what are deemed good uses. The prophets preach, but trust in their own insight—maybe informed by a nugget of psychological wisdom (Dr. Phil!) or a piece of social analysis (Noam Chomsky!)—without even expecting that the faith might have anything distinct to say about the matter. Wittingly or unwittingly, a serious malfunction has occurred—provided we understand the Christian faith not just as a version of some generic moral teaching, but as a prophetic *faith* in the Creator, Redeemer, and Consummator of the world.

In the famous passage in *The Gay Science* about the murder of God—not the death of God, but the *murder* of God!—Nietzsche describes churches unforgettably as "tombs and sepulchers of God."[8] In an important sense (though not the one Nietzsche had in mind), that is what churches and religious language become

10

when the pretense of ascent—functional reduction—occurs: with the prophets having abandoned the living God, churches and religious language morph into locations where God may have once been active, shaping people and their social realities, but in which God now lies dead, no longer a transformative reality, alive only as a topographic memory.

Idolatric Substitution

The second ascent malfunction is *idolatric substitution.*[9] Much in the Christian faith depends on properly identifying and discerning the will of the One in whose name the prophets are speaking and acting. But God dwells in unapproachable light, as the New Testament says (1 Tim. 6:16), and the sacred texts are notoriously difficult to interpret. Needing to engage the world in God's name and yet finding it difficult, uncomfortable, or even contrary to their deep-seated convictions to properly identify God and discern God's will, prophets sometimes transform God in their imagination into a caricature of the true divinity. The prophet's image of God occludes the reality of God and insinuates itself in its place. The error of idolatric substitution has occurred, and faith is poised to malfunction seriously.

Recall the paradigmatic case of idolatry in the Hebrew Scriptures, the story of the golden calf: Moses has ascended the mountain to be with God and receive from God "tablets of stone, with the law and the commandment" for the instruction of the people (Exod. 24:12). The Israelites find it hard to wait for Moses to return, so they push Aaron to make for them gods "who shall go before us" (Exod. 32:1). Aaron collects gold from the Israelites to "cast an image of a calf" as their god (Exod. 32:4). As Moses comes down the mountain, carrying the tablets of stone inscribed by the finger of God, he becomes furious at the betrayal. The Israelites have substituted the golden calf for Yahweh, who delivered them from Egypt.

Imagine now a different scene. Aaron and the Israelites are patiently and faithfully waiting for Moses to return. Finally, they see him coming down. But rather than tablets of stone, he carries the golden calf. And then they hear him speak: "These are your gods, O Israel, who brought you up out of the land of Egypt" (Exod. 32:4). The prophet himself would have now engaged in idolatric substitution. He ascended the mountain to meet with God, but he has returned with an idol. Impossible? It happens every day, and to the best of ordinary prophets, even if it does not happen in such a crass way: the prophets may carry down from the mountain the tablets of stone, but at least some of the writing on them can be traced to the golden calf rather than to the true God of Israel. For instance, sometimes, by some strange alchemy, "Take up your cross and follow me" morphs into "I'll bring out the champion in you,"[10] or the cross itself becomes a symbol of destruction and violence rather than of creative love that overcomes enmity.

Return Malfunctions

Every ascent malfunction is at the same time a return malfunction. Whether prophets pretend ascent to the mountain of God or descend from the mountain with what looks like God's word but is in fact a message from the golden calf, the *return* too has been compromised. The prophets may be transforming the world, but God is not involved in the transformation; they are transforming it in their own name or in the name of some alien god.

There are, however, other malfunctions of faith that don't primarily concern ascent but still threaten the integrity of the return. These "return malfunctions" come primarily in two forms: idleness of faith and coerciveness of faith, and they correspond roughly to the two kinds of sins categorized in Christian tradition: sins of omission, in which we fail to do what we should do, and sins of commission, in which we do what we should not do.[11] In this book I am concerned primarily with idleness and oppressiveness of faith, which I will discuss in chapters 2 and 3, respectively. I present these concepts here in order to introduce them and situate them within the larger framework of malfunctions of the Christian faith as a prophetic religion.

Idleness of Faith

The first return malfunction is *idleness of faith*. A major purpose of the Christian faith is to shape the lives of persons and communities. Yet faith often idles in many spheres of life, spinning in one place like the wheel of a car stuck in the snow. Granted, faith's idleness is never total—if it were total, faith would soon be discarded, for the faith that does nothing means nothing.

Sometimes faith idles because of the *lure of temptation*. Even people committed to high moral standards succumb to temptation: fraud in business, infidelity in marriage, plagiarism in scholarly work, abuse of priestly authority, or a host of other wrongs. Faith requires Christians to live lives of integrity, but we find ourselves powerless against the lure of evil. Finite, fragile, and fallible as we are, we easily succumb to the seductions of power, possessions, or glory.

Giving in is as old as humanity—but so is victory over temptation. To live with integrity, it is important to know what's right and what's wrong, to be educated morally. However, merely *knowing* is not enough. Virtuous character matters more than moral knowledge. The reason is simple: like the self-confessing apostle Paul in Romans 7, most of those who do wrong know what's right but find themselves irresistibly attracted to its opposite. Faith idles when character shrivels.

Perhaps even more often in our modern world, faith idles as a result of the *power of systems*. The lure of temptation is amplified by the power of the systems that surround us and in which we play a part. So it is in most spheres of life, but maybe most of all in the nearly ubiquitous market, whether that be the market of ideas, goods and services, political influence, or mass communication.

More than a century ago, Max Weber ended his classic *The Protestant Ethic and the Spirit of Capitalism* by speaking of the modern market as an "iron cage."[12] What he had in mind is roughly something like this: if you play the game, you've got to play it by preset rules, which in the case of the market means that you must maximize profit; these rules, and not moral considerations, determine how the game is played. The market traps you, compelling you to act in accordance with its rules. Others have suggested that large-scale bureaucratic arrangements function similarly.[13] A soldier in a unit, for example, is often willing to do what he would never do as a private person. He is simply obeying orders, or he assumes a role ascribed to him by the system.[14]

In such situations, faith may not completely fail to shape the lives of people and their social realities. Instead, its work might get restricted to a narrow sphere—to the life of the soul, to private morality, to family matters, or to church life. As a result, faith becomes idle in important domains in which it, as a prophetic faith, should be active.

That faith's sphere of operation often gets restricted is not surprising, especially under the conditions of modernity. The modern world, differentiated as it is into multiple and relatively autonomous spheres, is a world of many gods.[15] Each sphere— be it politics, law, business, media, or whatever—imposes its own rules upon those who wish to participate in it. In this new polytheism, we follow the voice of one god at work, another at home, and maybe yet another at church. Each sphere resists the claims of the one God to shape all of life.[16]

Most people of faith living in the modern world have experienced this pull of divided loyalties. Though many have given in, many others have also resisted. Those who resist have refused to play the game when the rules conflict with their deeply held religious convictions. They have tried to transform their places of work from within, endeavored to create more just rules of engagement, and sometimes even worked to set up alternative institutions so that the demands of their work can stay in sync with the claims of their faith. Why? Because they know they must be people of faith not only in the inner sanctuary of their souls, in their private lives, or when gathered with like-minded folks in the church, but also in their everyday activities, in the various places in which they do their daily work.

Idleness of faith might also arise from a *misconstrual of faith*. A misunderstanding of how our faith should function can provide fertile ground both for the lure of temptation and the power of systems. In some such situations, faith fails to shape realities at all but instead provides some other benefit to the worshiper. In his early text, somewhat cumbersomely titled "Towards a Critique of Hegel's *Philosophy of Right*," the young Karl Marx famously noted that religion—the Christian faith, he meant primarily—is "the opiate of the people."[17] It's a drug, and it's a "downer" or "depressant" insulating people from the pain of oppressive social realities and consoling them with a dream world of heavenly bliss. Alternatively, religion can function as an "upper," a "stimulant" energizing people for the tasks at hand—a function of religion Marx failed to grasp.

But the most important point Marx missed is that when Christian faith functions only as a soothing or performance-enhancing drug, faith is in fact *mal*functioning. This mistake is not unique to Marx or to Christianity's critics more generally. Many of those who have embraced faith have missed that all-important point too, from at least the time of the Old Testament prophets to today. Such people have themselves used faith more or less as a drug. Faith thus construed is, in a crucial sense, idling and can effect no transformation of personal or social lives.

Notice that I write that faith malfunctions when it serves *only* to soothe—or maybe more broadly, to heal—and to energize. In the Christian Bible there are two great traditions that very roughly cover these two functions of faith. These are the traditions of "deliverance" and of "blessing." Faith helps repair broken bodies and souls, including healing the wounds and disappointments inflicted on us in the rough and tumble of the everyday world. Faith also helps energize us so we can perform our tasks excellently, with requisite power, concentration, and creativity (see chapter 2).

So why speak of faith's malfunctioning in this regard? Let me put it this way: if faith *only* heals and energizes, then it is merely a crutch to use at will, not a way of life. But the Christian faith, as a prophetic religion, is either a way of life or a parody of itself. Put starkly and with echoes of the Epistle of James, an idle faith is no Christian faith at all.

Faith does its most proper work when it (1) sets us on a journey, (2) guides us along the way, and (3) gives meaning to each step we take. When we embrace faith—when *God* embraces *us*—we become new creatures constituted and called to be part of the people of God. That is the beginning of a journey: our insertion into the story of God's engagement with humanity. As we embark upon it, faith guides us by offering itself as a way of life that indicates paths to be taken and dark alleys or dead-end streets to be avoided, and that tells us what our specific tasks are in the great story of which we are a part. Finally, that story itself gives meaning to all we do, from the smallest act to the weightiest. Is what we do in concord with that story? Then it is meaningful and will remain, glistening as corrosion-resistant gold. Does it clash with the story? Then it is ultimately meaningless and will burn like straw, even if we find it the most thrilling and fulfilling activity in which we've ever engaged.

For Christian faith not to be idle in the world, the work of medical doctors and garbage collectors, business executives and artists, stay-at-home parents and scientists needs to be inserted into God's story of the world. That story needs to provide the most basic rules by which the "game" in all these spheres is played. And that story needs to shape the character of the players.

Coerciveness of Faith

The second return malfunction is *coerciveness of faith*. In this case, faith is not idle but active—hyperactive, in fact—imposing itself oppressively upon the unwilling. Often in the modern world Christian traditions oscillate between the two return malfunctions. Wanting to overcome idleness, faith becomes coercive; wanting to avoid coerciveness, faith becomes idle.

Sometimes a prophetic faith will be experienced as oppressive even when it may not be oppressive. Those who affirm contemporary social "polytheism" will deem oppressive any faith that claims that God is the God of all reality, and they will do so no matter how that faith tries to bring God to bear on all aspects of life. For instance, they may want religious folks to leave their religious garb—their sacred texts and reasoning based on religious convictions—at home or in the church and put on secular attire at the workplace or in the public square. If they refuse to wear the attire proper to the occasion, they are perceived as shoving religion down people's throats. From the perspective of people who believe that faith should shape their vision of human flourishing and of the common good, speaking in a religious voice is not oppressive but salutary; they would betray themselves and make their faith malfunction if they were silent or did not give religious reasons for their positions.[18] And advocates of a prophetic faith will view attempts to prevent them from living out their faith in private and public as secularism being shoved down their throats.

While the mere fact of speaking in a religious voice in the public arena is not oppressive, the *way* religious people bring faith to bear on issues of common concern can be, and often is, oppressive. The adherents of prophetic religion might set goals for themselves (say, a preemptive military strike), and then use faith to legitimize ignoble means to achieve them (say, by claiming the enemies believe in an evil God and are therefore evil people).[19] More frequently, the adherents of prophetic religion will let faith dictate the ends to be achieved (say, protecting unborn life or abolishing the death penalty), but fail to allow faith to determine the means to achieve those ends (opponents are not even respected, let alone treated with benevolence and beneficence). In all such cases—and many more—faith malfunctions by becoming an instrument of oppression.

Mostly it's Christians who worry about the idleness of their own faith. For them faith is a precious good, the most valuable personal and social resource. When it's left untapped, human beings cannot properly flourish, and the common good—not just the particular interests of Christians—suffers. In contrast, many non-Christians today would consider the idleness of faith a minor blessing. *Active* faith is dangerous, they believe, and inherently poisonous. As a recent critic, Sam Harris, puts it in *The End of Faith*, the Bible contains "mountains of life-destroying gibberish."[20] When Christians take the Bible as their final authority, Harris claims, they act in violent, oppressive, life-destroying ways that undermine the common good.

Take, for instance, a Serbian soldier riding on a tank and triumphantly flashing three fingers in the air—a symbol of the most holy Trinity, a sign that he belongs to a group that believes rightly about God. Clearly he has employed faith, in some sense, to give legitimacy to his triumphant ride on that killing machine. And he is not alone in draping the wild-eyed god of war or the fierce goddess of nationhood with the legitimizing mantle of religious faith. Some of his Croatian enemies have done the same, as have many Americans who have eagerly merged the cross and the flag; and they all follow in the footsteps of Christians over the centuries who, in the name of faith, have left behind them a trail of blood and tears.

Some critics (as well as some seekers!) ask pointedly, however, "Isn't this simply what the Christian faith does?" Along with many in the highbrow culture of the post-Enlightenment West, they seek to eliminate faith as a factor in social life, possibly even to eradicate it fully. How should Christians respond? Certainly not by trying to deny the obvious—a long and deeply troubling history of the complicity of their faith in violence (even if such complicity is by no means the greater part of the Christian story)!

Instead, Christians should show how faith, though prone to misuse, is a salutary way of life and inculcate its vision of lives well lived in all spheres. But even if we accept that Christianity is at heart nonviolent and that, properly practiced, it contributes to rather than detracts from human flourishing, we may still ask ourselves: why have *Christians* so often been oppressive and violent? There are three main reasons, and they partly correspond to the three reasons for faith's idleness: thinned out faith (which corresponds to misconstrual of faith), seemingly irrelevant faith (which corresponds, roughly, to the power of the systems), and unwillingness to walk the narrow path (which corresponds to the lure of temptation).

First, a *thinned out faith*. I have already mentioned how a person might take faith as a source of energy or healing for the body and soul, but not as a guide for shaping a vision of human flourishing. Or a person might embrace the ends mandated by his or her faith (for some, for instance, maintaining the sanctity of unborn life or just social arrangements) but not the means by which faith demands that these ends be reached (persuasion rather than violence, since two wrongs don't make a right, as Socrates notes in the *Crito*).[21] This results in a thinned-out faith: faith is not allowed full sway in shaping the way Christians live, but is either employed to achieve goals set by values unrelated to faith or allowed to define goals but not the means of achieving them. If this is correct, then the cure for religiously induced violence is not less faith but *more* faith—faith in its full scope, faith enacted with integrity and courage by its holy men and women, faith pondered responsibly by its great theologians.

Second, a *seemingly irrelevant faith*. Why would those who embrace the Christian faith not want to embody its vision fully? Sometimes the original faith seems outdated, unworkable, irrelevant. Can a faith originally embraced by a minority—a sometimes persecuted minority, at that—tell us anything useful about governing, running a large business, or defending a nation from enemies? Can a faith born two thousand years ago have any relevance to democracies struggling with how to use their vast technological potential for the good of humanity rather than its self-destruction? Deep down, we fear that our faith may indeed be irrelevant; we sense a tension, so we bracket faith's moral vision and use faith merely to bless what we think is right to do in any case. It takes hard intellectual and spiritual work to understand and live faith authentically under changed circumstances. And it is the kind of work that cannot be placed only on the shoulders of theologians, but an endeavor in which academics engaged in a variety of scholarly disciplines and faithful people from all walks of life must be involved.

Third, an *unwillingness to walk the narrow path*. When someone has violated us or our community, we feel the urge for revenge—and we set aside the explicit command to love our enemies, to be benevolent and beneficent toward them. Or we believe that our culture is going down a perilous road and want to change its self-destructive course—but we forget that the ends that Christian faith holds high do not justify setting aside its strictures about appropriate means. Or we see immense potential for healing debilitating and painful maladies in embryonic stem cell research—and we don't quite know how to think about the destruction of embryos that seems required if research should proceed successfully, so we bracket faith's demands in regard to this issue. We first deem the moral tug that our faith exerts on us to be impractical, then impractical slides into "overly demanding"—and eventually we reject what we once thought to be right as a course of action that is no longer viable. In these and many other ways, we mold faith to fit our own desires and our capacity to live in a given situation.

And so we are back to the question of character. In addition to applying an authentically understood faith to various spheres of life, we need properly formed persons who resist misusing faith in oppressive ways. For the Christian, faith produces devastating results when it devolves into a mere personal or cultural resource for people whose lives are guided by anything but that faith.

2

Idleness

I dleness, I argued in the previous chapter, is one major malfunction of faith. Instead of setting goals and propelling a person toward them, idle faith spins in one place, like a tire stuck in an icy hole. I suggested that there are at least three reasons for faith's idling. The first concerns the character of believers; for some people, the faith they embrace demands too much, so they pick and choose, as in a cafeteria, filling up their tray with sweets but leaving aside the broccoli and fish. Second, believers find themselves constrained by large and small systems in which they live and work; to thrive, or even to survive, they feel that they must obey the logic of those systems, not the demands of faith they embrace. The third reason for faith's idleness concerns the faith itself; the faith either is not applied to new circumstances or does not seem relevant to contemporary issues—from nuclear power to neuroscientific discoveries. With these three reasons for faith's idleness combined, no wonder people misconceive faith and treat it as a

23

performance-enhancing drug or a soothing balm rather than as a resource to orient their life in the world.

In this chapter, I will suggest how to understand and practice an active faith. I will examine four basic ways that faith relates to our daily life—to our everyday work, very broadly conceived. These ways are closely related to four basic questions we ask as we engage in any activity. (1) How do I succeed? (2) How do I cope with failure? (3) What should I do and what can I leave undone? (4) Why should I engage in the activity in the first place?

Blessing

In all our activities, and certainly in all our work, we strive to succeed. By this I mean that we want to (1) accomplish what we have undertaken to do, (2) accomplish it in an excellent way, and, hopefully, (3) contribute to some larger good. In addition to our native ability and training, to succeed we first need something that can be roughly described as *power*—an ability to exert continued effort, to give our projects sustained attention and focus, and to perform in critical situations. Second, to succeed we often need *creativity*—an ability to imagine new things and to find new ways of doing old things. Creativity is particularly important in today's fast-paced and highly competitive cultures, which place great stock in novelty.

We need power and creativity to succeed, but we inhabit a fragile and uncertain world and are ourselves fragile and unpredictable creatures. This is the metaphysical condition under which we live. Our will does not always master our activity or its outcome. We get tired and depleted; we become distracted, and our attention scatters; we make a big mistake under the pressure of a critical situation. Moreover, even when we've done all that we could, input does not guarantee outcome. Hard work isn't always crowned with success because sometimes the unexpected and the unwelcome intervene. Or maybe we burn the midnight oil, but no bright idea arrives.

Since power and creativity are in short supply, to succeed we often seek the help of what we describe as the "higher power." Athletes pray in critical situations, students pray during exams, high-stakes negotiators pray before approaching major deals. The sophisticated among us sometimes dismiss such prayers. First, the concerns that give rise to them seem petty in the larger scheme of things. Does God really care which team wins or what grade I get? Second, we worry that such prayers entail misuse of faith. To enlist God's help in critical situations seems to reduce God to a performance-enhancing drug and, in effect, gives an unfair advantage to one side. Finally, some people may worry that such prayers reflect a misunderstanding of the relationship between God and the world. The prayers presuppose, one could argue, a "God-of-the-results" account of that relationship. You pray, and miraculously knowledge gets infused into your head, even though you haven't studied that hard. So prayer serves to shirk responsibility.

But despite such concerns, to which I will respond briefly in just a moment, it is important to connect God with success in work. The Scriptures make that connection rather consistently, especially in the tradition of God's blessing in the Hebrew Scriptures. In the Hebrew Scriptures there are, roughly, two kinds of blessings. First is the blessing of God's power as sustainer of the universe, by which God continuously upholds human life and enables its flourishing. That's what it means, for instance, for the whole human race to have been blessed at the dawn of creation (see Gen. 1:28).[1] Second, blessing is a very specific activity of God directed at a particular human undertaking. God crowns an effort with success, be it in procreation, business, or war (see Gen. 26:12–13).

If you walk into any large bookstore and look through the section on spirituality and work, you'll see that the main theme of most books is how to harness spiritual energies in order to succeed.[2] New Age "theologians" will tell a willing reader how to thrive, even beat the competition. In contrast, Christian theologians, especially in mainline denominations, have often tried to distance God from mundane success and instead concentrated on God's demands on us. As I'll note shortly, God's demands are extraordinarily important if faith is not to idle in some crucial regards, especially in today's climate in which we seem to be plagued by high-profile scandals in many spheres of life, from industry to journalism, science, politics, academics, and, most appallingly for Christians, ministry.

But fundamentally, God is not a demander; God is a giver.[3] That is what the tradition of blessing revealed in the Hebrew Scriptures brings to expression. God's generosity holds true not just in the realm of salvation, when the well-being of our souls is at stake. It also holds true in the realm of creation and therefore in the realm of everyday activities. If God is the source of our being, then we do all our work in the power that comes from God. God gives, and therefore we exist and can work. God gives, and therefore we can succeed in our work.

Our endeavors are at times misguided and need to be corrected, such as when we want to succeed at the others' expense. We may inappropriately desire that God act in our favor, as in athletic contests. (The team God helped would be cheating!) But none of our endeavors and concerns are too small for God. God wants to empower us to succeed. God is the power of our being and therefore also the power of our succeeding. Moreover, our mundane work is part of our service to God. It is God who sustains us; it is God who gives us power and creativity; and it is ultimately God for whom we work. Hence it is quite appropriate to ask God to bless our endeavors.

26

In asking God to help us succeed, though, are we not abdicating some of our own responsibility? We would be if receiving God's blessing meant that God did things that otherwise we would have to do. But that's not the case. When God blesses, God does not create finished products; God works through human means to achieve God's ends. With regard to our success in work, we pray not so much for God to miraculously bring about a desired result but to make us willing, capable, and effective instruments in God's hand—which is what we were created to be in the first place.[4]

Deliverance

The second way in which faith makes a difference instead of just idling has to do with breakdowns—with failures in our work. None of us like to admit to failures. We design our lives to keep failure at bay and, when failure strikes, to make it invisible. As a result, it is difficult for us to think of ourselves as having failed. Yet when we work, we are always in danger of some sort of failure, and we are often deeply troubled by the failures we experience. We need help not only to succeed but also after we have failed.

Breakdowns occur in spite of our precautions; we fall sick at a critical time, get injured at work, and so on. We fail to achieve our goals in spite of our best efforts; we work hard and nonetheless get a bad grade, get fired from a job, or lose a big deal to a competitor. It's even tougher when we do the right thing, and precisely because of that, we fail. Then there is the failure that lies within success itself. We have climbed to the top, and we still feel deeply dissatisfied; like cold mist, melancholy envelops our very success. In a finite, fragile, and highly competitive world, failure is always a threat.

When people fail and things break down, they often turn to faith. A critic may object once again: If you come to God in your failure, don't you reduce God to a servant of your need? If in success God functions as a divine performance-enhancing drug, doesn't God function in failure as a divine Band-Aid? But if God is concerned about us, God will both empower us to succeed (as well as define for us what success means!) and help us when we fail.

In the Hebrew Scriptures, along with the tradition of God's blessing, there is also the tradition of God's *deliverance* (see Exod. 14:10–13; Ps. 65:5; Isa. 51:6–8).[5] At the heart of the tradition of deliverance, we find, maybe surprisingly, the problem of human work. Liberation from slave labor in Egypt was the defining act of God's redemption for the people of Israel. Cruel taskmasters oppressed the people of Israel, and God redeemed them. So to a large extent, the exodus of the children of Abraham and Sarah from Egypt is redemption from bad work.

Consider, first, our frequent failure in spite of integrity. How does faith make a difference? God promises that if we do what is right, *ultimately* we cannot fail to achieve happiness or to succeed in the most comprehensive sense of that term. We are often puzzled as to why we should do what is morally good—and not just for the sake of a benefit we get from it—when those who do evil often thrive. Immanuel Kant's response was that it makes sense for people to do good for the sake of the good itself only if the world is set up in such a way that you don't have to act immorally in order to be ultimately happy.[6] He concluded that only God can be the source of such a world; only God can ensure that virtuous living and happiness ultimately match.

Second, even when we fail, whether we have done our best or were unable to do our best, God gives us a sense of worth beyond our successes and failures. True, work is part and parcel of our identity.[7] Who we are is shaped in part by the kind of work we do and the kind of workers we are. But we are more, much more, than our work because we are the beloved

28

children of God both in success and in failure. God does not love us because of our success, and God does not cease to love us when we fail. When it comes to our sense of dignity, God's love trumps everything else.[8]

Finally, God delivers us from the melancholy emptiness that sometimes accompanies our very success. We've achieved what we wanted—we have gotten the corner office—and we still feel empty. We are like a child who wants a toy and, when she gets it, plays with it for a day or two and then craves another. Melancholy inevitably sets in when we forget that we are made to find satisfaction in the infinite God and not in any finite object.[9] It also sets in if we work just for ourselves and don't see our work as a service to a community and as part of God's ongoing engagement with creation. I will return to this idea when I address the relationship between God and meaning.

Interlude: Idleness and Misdirected Busyness

The two functions of faith examined so far are significant in their own right, and yet if we stopped with them, they would morph into malfunctions of faith—at least when it comes to prophetic faiths. Faith's functions would be reduced, roughly, to energizing and repairing; faith would not orient in any significant way how people live in the world. In a crucial sense, faith would be still idling, because prophetic faiths should be a way of life, not just a "religious" resource for a way of life whose content is shaped by factors outside of that faith itself (such as national security, economic prosperity, or our thirst for pleasure, power, and glory). In another sense, of course, faith that only blessed and redeemed would be busy—busy problematically blessing and redeeming that which, from the perspective of that faith itself, should not be blessed and should not be redeemed. This is how idleness of faith prepares the way for the coerciveness of faith—a malfunction I will address in the following chapter. A faith that makes a difference authentically is a faith that guides what we do in the world and that shapes how we understand the world and our place in it.

Guidance

How does faith guide what we should do? Applied to work broadly conceived, the question has a moral side—what kind of work is morally permissible and commendable?—as well as a personal side—into what should we pour our energies, and how should we employ our talents?[10] Let me address here only the moral side of the question. It is clearly more fundamental, for we cannot be called and gifted by God to do anything morally impermissible.

We may not be particularly attracted to being garbage collectors, but from a moral standpoint, it's a fine kind of work as well as a communal necessity. Other types of work, however, are morally unacceptable. Even if I could earn a ton of money, I should never be a hired killer; or even if I deem a cause good, I may not become a terrorist to further it. But there are some types of work that may be ambiguous. Is it morally permissible to produce, market, and sell assault weapons or sex toys (to mention products that concern two of the most powerful human urges)? Is it morally permissible to work in an industry that excessively pollutes the environment?[11]

Maybe even more important is discernment *within* morally acceptable types of work. Recall an important distinction that is often made in just war theory between the just resort to war (*ius ad bellum*) and the just conduct of war (*ius in bello*).[12] According to proponents of just war theory, a nation can have a just cause for war and yet conduct the war unjustly. The same applies to all our work, not just the work of waging war. Within a type of work that is morally acceptable, we still need to decide what is ethical and what is not, and act accordingly. The larger setting within which we work—whether that is a company, an industry, or the whole market—will exert pressure on us to achieve success as measured by its standards. And yet, if we don't want to hang our faith on the coatrack at the entrance of our workplace, we will have to let faith have the final word as to what we should or should not do.

Notice that the moral guidance offered by faith differs from legal constraints within a given polity. Laws are designed partly to protect the public from unscrupulous individuals and institutions. Yet as important as legal constraints are, they are not sufficient on their own. The fact that something is legal doesn't mean that it's moral. The moral question is the question of right versus wrong, not simply the question of legal versus illegal, though, of course, these two issues often overlap. It is legal to run companies that use child labor in impoverished countries just as it is in many places legal to seriously pollute the environment. But is it moral to do so? There are, of course, gray zones when it comes to moral issues, and sometimes no matter what we do, it seems we are going to overstep the boundary of what is morally good.

Finally, a properly functioning faith nudges us to go beyond what is morally permissible and do what is morally *excellent*. Some years ago at a black-tie cocktail party, I was talking to a person who introduced himself to me as a graduate of Harvard University. We were chatting, so I asked him what he did. He responded, "You will laugh when I tell you what I do." I said, "Well, try me." He replied, "I'm making urinals." I said, "Well, most men need them . . ." And he responded, "I'm designing and producing flush-free urinals." What an extraordinary thing to do! Water is becoming a very scarce resource, and he was helping save a lot of it, in fact some forty thousand gallons per urinal per year! This person's work was morally excellent, not just morally permissible.

A faith that makes a difference is a faith that helps us discern and motivates us to do what is right and excellent. Some Christians keep God out of the moral dimension of their work lives. They believe that God saves souls and directs private morality, that God even enhances performance and heals wounds. God seems detached, though, from the moral decisions we face in our more public lives. When we limit God to the private sphere rather than letting God shape our entire lives, a prophetic faith fails to do some of its most important work. In one of its crucial functions, it idles. And what's worse, idling in this regard makes it malfunction as a source of blessing and deliverance.

Meaning

It is not enough for us to achieve success and avoid failure, not even to do so while leading lives of moral integrity and excellence. We are human in part because when we work or when we play, we don't "just do it" (as the Nike commercial of some years ago put it). We *reflect* on the meaning of what we do, asking the question, to what end do we do what we do? We also reflect on whether our answers to the "why" question make sense. Is the purpose for which I work sufficient to sustain me over time not just as an "economic animal," but as a human being? Is it in sync with the nature of reality—with who I am as a bodily, spiritual, and communal being, and with how the world is made up?[13] The faith that makes a difference will provide plausible answers to these questions. Indeed, that is its most important function.

There are many possible ways of construing the meaning of work. One purpose that immediately comes to mind is to put bread on the table—and a car into the garage or an art object into the living room, some may add. Put more abstractly, the purpose of work is to take care of the needs of the person who does it. Often we strive after things not so much because we need them in any strong sense of that term, nor even because they make life easier for us and give us pleasure, but because we want to have more and better things than our neighbors. Work and the things work procures then serve to boost our self-image and define our success. "The one with the most toys wins."

But when we consider taking care of ourselves as the main purpose of work, we unwittingly get stuck on the spinning wheel of dissatisfaction. What we possess always lags behind what we desire, and so we become victims of Lewis Carroll's curse, "Here, you see, it takes all the running you can do to keep in the same place."[14] In our quiet moments, we know that we want our lives to have weight and substance and to grow toward some kind of fullness that lies beyond ourselves. Our own selves, and especially the pleasures of our own selves, are insufficient to give meaning to our lives. When the meaning of work is reduced to the well-being of the working self, the result is a feeling of melancholy and unfulfillment, even in the midst of apparent success.

A second purpose of work is the flourishing of communities. We are communal beings. We live from community, and even the most "self-made" individual has been influenced significantly by others; he has had a mother and a father, he has had a teacher, he has had a culture with its practices, institutions, traditions. And because we are such communal beings, we find the meaning of work in community. That community can be a family whose needs we seek to meet, a corporation for whose success we work, an ecclesiastical community to whose mission we want to contribute, a civic community whose vibrancy we strive to sustain, or even a world community.

When we work for the well-being of communities, our work acquires a richer texture of meaning than when we work just for ourselves. We are then not only self-seeking; we are living for

33

the benefit of others. And as we read in Scripture, "It is more blessed to give than to receive" (Acts 20:35). A faith that makes a difference nudges us to work out of love not just for ourselves but for our near and distant neighbors as well.

Yet it is not clear that even concern for a community's well-being is substantial enough to give our work and our lives their proper meaning. If our own well-being and the well-being of community are all there is to working, would not our working in some sense be like building sandcastles on the seashore? It is meaningful as long as the activity and its results last, but it's ultimately futile. A tide comes and washes away all the hard work, leaving no trace of it. If there were no more to our work than the benefit to ourselves and our communities, rapacious time would swallow us and the fruits of our labor, and our work would remain ultimately meaningless.[15] Our work can find its ultimate meaning when, in working for ourselves and for community, we work for God.

What is the relationship of God to the meaning of our work? There are four major ways in which God relates to the meaning of work. First, God is, in a sense, our *employer*. As we strive to satisfy our own needs and contribute to the well-being of the community, we work for God, we serve God. Here God gives us tasks to do in the world—commands us to have dominion over the world (Gen. 1) or to "keep and till" the garden (Gen. 2)—and we do what God commands.

Second, we can think of our work as not just fulfilling God's commands but achieving God's *purposes* in the world. In Matthew's Gospel, when describing the judgment of the nations, Jesus says to the sheep at his right, "Come, you that are blessed by my Father, inherit the kingdom prepared for you from the foundation of the world; for I was hungry and you gave me food, I was thirsty and you gave me something to drink, I was a stranger and you welcomed me, I was naked and you gave me clothing, I was sick and you took care of me, I was in prison and you visited me" (Matt. 25:34–36). Whatever the "sheep" did to the least members of Jesus's family, they did it to him. God loves creation and all creatures, and when we care for their well-being, we work for God's purposes and in this way also for God.

Third, in our work we *cooperate* with God, and that gives meaning to our work. Consider the second account of creation in which, in the form of a story, God's original purpose with humanity is laid bare (Gen. 2:4–25). It starts with the statement that there was no vegetation on earth after God created it. Two reasons are given for this: first, God had not yet let rain fall on the ground, and second, human beings were not around to till it. Only when human beings come onto the scene and start working can God's work of creation be completed. God creates, God preserves, God's blessing is enacted, God transforms the world in anticipation of the world to come—and in all that, God makes us God's own coworkers.[16] We work with God, and God works through us. We make decisions in boardrooms, we flip hamburgers at McDonald's, we clean houses, we drive buses, we publish books and deliver lectures—and by doing that, we work with God and God works through us. No greater dignity could be assigned to our work.

Finally, God makes sure that none of what is true, good, and beautiful in our work will be lost. In God, everything that we have done in cooperation with God will be preserved. In the world to come, our work will not disappear. We ourselves will be followed by our works, as it says in the book of Revelation (14:13). That makes sense if our identity partly resides in our work and its achievements. Even in the world to come, I could not meet Gutenberg and not think of the printing press, or meet Einstein and not think of his theory of relativity, or meet the apostle Paul and not think of the Epistle to the Romans. The results of our work—the cumulative results of generations of workers across the globe—will also be preserved in the world to come.[17] They may be preserved just in God's memory, or they may be preserved as actual building blocks of that new world.

The work of each one of us is, then, a small contribution to the grand tapestry of life, which God is weaving as God created the world, is redeeming the world, and will consummate the world. This is the ultimate meaning of our work.

Conclusion: On Doing Our Work Well

Here, then, are the contours of a faith that refuses to be idle: God blesses us, and we succeed in work; God delivers us so that we aren't weighed down by our failures and can achieve lasting happiness; God directs us so we can work in morally responsible and morally excellent ways; and God gives meaning to our work in that God gathers all our efforts on behalf of ourselves and our communities and works through them to create, redeem, and consummate the world. Our faith will make a positive difference when God is at work in our work in these four ways.

3

Coerciveness

I n the aftermath of the terrorist attacks on the World Trade Center it was not unusual to hear that the attack "changed everything." "Everything" is certainly an exaggeration, but 9/11, as the terrorist attacks are sometimes called, did change a good many things, including the attitudes of many secular Westerners toward religion. The attacks, in which more than three thousand lives were lost and which triggered two major wars (in Afghanistan and Iraq), were in part motivated by religion. What careful analysts and people all around the globe had known for some time suddenly became clear to secular Westerners: religion is very much alive today, and it is a force not only in the private but also the public lives of people in the world. For some years now a collection of essays entitled *Religion, the Missing Dimension of Statecraft* (which, when originally published in 1994, was seen as pushing the boundaries of its discipline) has become obligatory reading for diplomats in many countries, Western and non-Western.[1]

Eliminate Religion?

Mainstream sociologists of the twentieth century, who followed in the footsteps of Karl Marx, Max Weber, and Emile Durkheim, had predicted that religion would slowly wither away or lodge itself quietly into the privacy of worshipers' hearts. Instead, religion has emerged as an important player on the national and international scenes. It is too early to tell how permanent this resurgence of religion will be. The processes of secularization may continue (as seen in Continental Europe), though this is likely not in the sense of an overall decline of religious observance but rather in the sense of the diminishing influence of religion in contemporary societies. If secularization progresses, the problem of idleness may turn out to be more significant than the problem of faith's inappropriate assertiveness. Nevertheless, religion is presently alive and well on the public scene and will continue to be so in the foreseeable future.

In many people's minds, the reassertion of religion as a political factor has not been for the good. It seems that the gods have mainly terror on their minds, as the title of Mark Jurgensmeyer's book on the global rise of religious violence suggests: *Terror in the Mind of God.*[2] Among the intellectual elite in the Western cultural milieu, the contemporary coupling of religion and violence feeds on the mostly submerged memories of the wars that plagued Europe from the 1560s to the 1650s, in which religion, it is claimed, was "the burning motivation, the one that inspired fanatical devotion and the most vicious hatred."[3] It was these wars that contributed a great deal to the emergence of secularizing modernity.[4]

Like key Enlightenment figures, many contemporaries see religion as a pernicious social ill that requires aggressive treatment rather than considering it a medicine from which a cure can be expected. Did not the perpetrators of the 9/11 terrorist attacks appeal to religion as motivation for their violence? In the recent war in the Balkans, did not the Serbs fight for the land on which the holy sites of their religion stood? Was not difference between Catholicism and Protestantism at the heart of the civil war in Northern Ireland? Is not religion a major factor in clashes in India? The contemporary resurgence of religion seems to go hand in hand with the resurgence of religiously legitimized violence—at least in the public perception. For this reason, many argue that it is necessary to weaken, neutralize, or eliminate religion outright as a factor in public life.

The impulse to neutralize or eliminate religion from public space is mistaken, however. It is mistaken because it is hardly possible to eliminate religion without violence—violence now toward religious folks for whom religion defines a way of life, private as well as public. The impulse to eliminate religion is mistaken also because religions can and often do play an indispensable role in fostering healthy and peaceful social relations. These are bold claims that I will leave here unexamined. In the present chapter I will undertake a more modest task: I will contest the claim that the Christian faith predominantly fosters violence. This too may seem a bold claim. Lest I be misunderstood, let me clarify it.

Thin and Thick Faith

First, I will not argue that the Christian faith was never violent or that it does not continue to be employed to foster violence. Obviously, such an argument cannot be plausibly made. Not only have Christians committed atrocities and engaged in less egregious forms of violence during the course of their long history, but they have also drawn on religious convictions to justify those acts.[5] Moreover, there are elements in the Christian faith that, when taken in isolation or when excessively foregrounded, can be used to legitimize violence. Second, I will not argue that

Christianity has been historically less associated with violence than other major religions. I am not sure whether this is or is not the case, and I am not sure how one would go about deciding the issue.

What I will argue is that, at least when it comes to Christianity, the cure against religiously induced and legitimized violence is almost exactly the opposite of what an important intellectual current in the West since the Enlightenment has been suggesting. The cure against Christian violence is not less of the Christian faith, but, in a carefully qualified sense, *more* of the Christian faith. I don't mean, of course, that the cure against violence lies in increased religious zeal; blind religious zeal is part of the problem. Instead, it lies in stronger and more intelligent commitment to the Christian faith as faith.

In terms of how Christian faith is conceived and practiced, my thesis is this: The more we reduce faith to vague religiosity that serves primarily to energize, heal, and give meaning to the business of life whose course is shaped by factors other than faith (such as national or economic interests), the worse off we will be. Inversely, the more the Christian faith matters to its adherents as faith that maps a way of life, and the more they practice it as an ongoing tradition with strong ties to its origins and history, and with clear cognitive and moral content, the better off we will be. "Thin" but zealous practice of the Christian faith is likely to foster violence; "thick" and committed practice will help generate and sustain a culture of peace.[6] This thesis claims that approaching the issue of religion and violence by looking at the *quantity* of religious attachments—more religion, more violence; less religion, less violence—is unsophisticated and mistaken. The most relevant factor is, rather, the *quality* of religious commitments.

In the present chapter I will respond to some influential arguments about the violent character of Christianity in order to support the claim that the Christian faith seriously malfunctions when it legitimizes violence. This is only half of what I would need to do to make my thesis plausible, a negative half. The other, positive half would be to show that at Christianity's heart, and not just at its margins, lie important resources for creating and sustaining a culture of peace.[7]

In the past, scholars have argued in a variety of ways that the Christian faith fosters violence. In a representative way I will engage four arguments that, in my estimation, go to the heart of the matter.[8]

Monotheism

Some scholars, such as Regina Schwartz in her book *The Curse of Cain: The Violent Legacy of Monotheism*, argue for the Christian faith's complicity in violence by pointing to the fact that, along with Judaism and Islam, Christianity is a monotheistic religion and therefore an exclusive and violent religion. "Whether as singleness (this God against the others) or totality (this is all the God there is), monotheism abhors, reviles, rejects, and ejects whatever it defines as outside its compass," Schwartz argues.[9] Given that the belief in one God "forges identity antithetically," religious commitment to the one God issues in a mistaken notion of identity ("we are 'us' because we are not 'them'") and contributes to violent practice ("we can remain 'us' only if we obliterate 'them'").

In addition, monotheism imports the category of universal "truth" into the religious sphere.[10] Along with many others, Željko Mardešić, a Croatian sociologist of religion, has noted that this fact lies at the heart of monotheism's exclusivity. To believe that there is only one God means to believe in the only *true* God. Moreover, since such a claim to truth about the moral and metaphysical character of the one God must be universal, it is inescapably public. Universal public claims cause strife when

41

they encounter opposing claims, of either a particular or a universal sort. For this reason too, monotheism is bound to have a violent legacy, the argument goes.[11] "We," the faithful, have on our side the one true God and stand in opposition to "them," the infidels and renegades.

It is not clear, however, that an affirmation of divine oneness *as such* leads to violence. Does not God's oneness work also against the tendency to divide people into "us" and "them"? If one accepts the belief in one God, in an important sense everybody is "in," and everybody is "in" precisely on the same terms. True, "being in on the same terms" may feel like coercion if you don't want to be "in" or you want to be "in" on different terms. But take monotheism away, and the division and violence between "us" and "them" hardly disappear, and if "us" or "them" are religious, we each will appeal to our god to wage war. In a polytheistic context violence may reassert itself with even more force, because it will necessarily be justified by locally legitimized or arbitrary preferences, against which, in the absence of a divinity who overarches the parties, there now can be no higher court of appeal. Even if monotheism is taken vaguely and abstractly as belief in one God without further qualification, it is not clear that it is likely to generate more violence than polytheism or atheism.

None of the monotheistic religions espouse such vague and abstract monotheism, however. Specifically Christian monotheism contains a further important pressure against violence, especially violence caused by self-enclosed and exclusive identities of the type that Schwartz criticizes. For Christian monotheism is of a trinitarian kind.[12] What difference does trinitarianism make?[13] With respect to social relations, one of the most important aspects of the doctrine of the Trinity concerns notions of identity. To believe that the one God is the Father, the Son, and the Holy Spirit is to believe that the identity of the Father, for instance, cannot be understood apart from the Son and the Holy Spirit. The Father's identity is from the start defined by the Son and the Spirit, and therefore it is not undifferentiated and self-enclosed. One cannot say without qualification that the Father is not the Son or the Spirit because to be the Father means to have the Son and the Spirit present in oneself. The same holds true, of course, of the Son and the Spirit in relation to the Father and one another.

Moreover, the divine persons as non-self-enclosed identities are understood by the Christian tradition to form a perfect communion of love. The persons give themselves to each other and receive themselves from each other in love. None has to wrest anything from others, none has to impose anything on others, and none needs to secure oneself from the incursions of others. Far from being a life of violence, the life of the divine being is characterized by mutually uncoerced and welcomed generosity.

It would be difficult to argue that such monotheism fosters violence.[14] Instead, it grounds peace here and now in the "transcendental" realm, in the love and peacefulness of the divine being. The argument for inherent violence of Christianity's monotheism works only if one illegitimately reduces the "thick" religious description of God to naked oneness and then postulates such abstract oneness to be of decisive social significance. I do not dispute that such reduction in fact happens within the Christian community—but when it does, the Christian faith has seriously malfunctioned. Just to affirm God's naked oneness is a sign that the Christian faith has not been taken seriously enough, rather than that it is inherently violent.

Creation

So far I have argued that Christian faith may generate violence in its "thin" but not in its "thick" form—when a "thick" characterization of the divine being's differentiated and complex identity (whose nature is defined by love, freely given and received) is reduced to an undifferentiated "One." But what about the argument that some very "thick" and "concrete" Christian convictions foster violence? Central here are the convictions about the world's creation and final consummation.

It is a basic Christian claim that God created the world. In her influential book *Sexism and God-Talk* Rosemary Radford Ruether makes the observation that in the Hebrew Scriptures, the Creator is like an artisan working on material outside his own nature. God does so, she argues, by "a combination of male seminal and cultural power (word-act) that shapes it 'from above.'"[15] In such an account, creation is a result of an imposition of form on formless matter from outside by an alien force. Hence creation is an act of violence.

What is wrong with this account of creation? Everything— almost. Let's assume for a moment that we should take Genesis literally, that creation is best described as forming preexisting material (rather than "forming" being an image that points to an activity only analogous to ordinary forming). One would still have to argue that this material is "something," and that it is a specific kind of something, which deserves respect. But it is not clear at all that chaos, which according to this account of creation God formed, is a "something." And if the chaos were a "something," why would it not be something analogous to a boulder from which an artisan can fashion a sculpture? For all the sparks flying off his chisel, Michelangelo working on "David" can hardly be described as perpetrating violence. For the activity of "forming" to do violence, the entity that is formed must possess integrity of its own that demands respect. Now, if someone were to smash Michelangelo's "David" into pieces, this would be an act of violence. But such "smashing" bears no resemblance to the divine forming in Genesis.

On the whole, however, the Christian tradition has not understood creation as "forming." Instead, it has insisted that God the Creator is not a demiurge working on preexisting matter; God created *ex nihilo*, out of nothing. The consequences of this understanding of creation for its putative violent character are significant. As Rowan Williams puts it in *On Christian Theology*, when we say that God creates, we do not mean that God "imposes a definition" but that God "creates an identity." He continues, "Prior to God's word there is nothing to impose on."[16] From this it follows that creation is not the exercise of an alien power, indeed that it is not an exercise of power at all, understood in the usual sense. Williams writes,

> Power is exercised by x over y; but creation is not power, because it is not exercised on anything. We might, of course, want to say that creation presupposes a divine potentiality, or resourcefulness, or abundance of active life; and "power" can sometimes be used in those senses. But what creation emphatically isn't is any kind of imposition or manipulation: it is not God imposing on us divinely willed roles rather than the ones we "naturally" might have, or defining us out of our own system into God's. . . . And this implies that the Promethean myth of humanity struggling against God for its welfare and interests makes no sense: to be a creature cannot be to be a victim of an alien force.[17]

Creation, then, is not a coercive act. Indeed, one may even argue that short of understanding the world as God's creation, relationships between entities in the world, especially human beings, would be necessarily violent.[18] If identities are not created, then the boundaries between identities must emerge out of interchanges between these entities. And these interchanges themselves must then be described as violent, since boundaries—precisely because they are always contested—are arbitrary. Given scarce resources, boundaries will always be the products of power struggles, even if those power struggles take the form of negotiations. Moreover, no appeals for arbitration between the contending parties can be made to something that ultimately stands outside the power struggle.

Redemption

But what about the *new creation*? What about God's activity to redeem creation from the consequences of sin? Clearly, the new creation is not *creatio ex nihilo* (creation out of nothing) but *creatio ex vetere* (creation out of old creation). That "old" and "sinful" creation possesses integrity of its own (even if it is, according to the Christian faith, an integrity in tension with its true character), and can and does assert its will over against God. In redeeming the world, God intervenes into the existing sinful world in order to transform it into a world of perfect love. Is this intervention not violent, and does it therefore not generate violence on the part of human beings?

The most radical critique of redemptive divine engagement as violent and violence-inducing comes from poststructuralist thinkers. For them, any determinacy of the goal to be achieved by divine transformation of this world and any specificity about the agent of transformation already breeds violence. On their account, in order for what needs to *come*, in contrast to what *is*, not to be violent, it must always remain completely other and cannot be expressed as an "onto-theological or teleo-eschatological program or design."[19] As John Caputo, speaking in the voice of his teacher, Jacques Derrida, puts it, "If the Messiah ever actually showed up . . . that would ruin everything."[20] Any and every messiah is problematic because by necessity he and his program would potentially exclude something or someone. Hence the only acceptable goal of desirable change is "absolute hospitality," a posture of welcoming the stranger without any preconditions, just as the only acceptable engagement to achieve it is "radical and interminable, infinite . . . critique."[21]

"Absolute hospitality" seems generous and peaceful, until one remembers that unrepentant perpetrators and their un-healed victims would then have to sit around the same table and share a common home without adequate attention to the violation that has taken place. In one crucial regard, the idea ends up too close for comfort to the Nietzschean affirmation of life, in which a sacred "yes" is pronounced to all that is and in which "but thus I willed it" is said of all that was, with all the small and large horrors of history.[22] Absolute hospitality would in no way amount to the absence of violence. To the contrary, it would enthrone violence precisely under the guise of nonviolence because it would leave the violators unchanged and the consequences of violence unremedied. Hospitality can be absolute only once the world has been made into a world of love in which each person would be hospitable to all. In the world of injustice, deception, and violence, hospitality can be only conditional—even if the will to hospitality and the offer of hospitality remain unconditional.[23]

It takes radical change, and not just an act of indiscriminate acceptance, for the world to be made into a world of love. The Christian tradition has tied this change with the coming of the Messiah, the crucified and resurrected One, whose appearance in glory is still awaited. Is this messianic intervention violent? Does it sanction human violence? The answer is easy when it comes to the Messiah's first coming. Jesus Christ did not come into the world in order to conquer evildoers through an act of violence, but to die for them in self-giving love and thereby reconcile them to God. The outstretched arms of the suffering body on the cross qualify the whole of Christ's mission. He condemned the sin of humanity by taking it upon himself; and by bearing it, he freed humanity from its power and restored their communion with God. Though suffering on the cross is not all Christ did, the cross represents the decisive criterion for how all his work is to be understood.

Does the belief in the Crucified generate violence? Beginning at least with Emperor Constantine's conversion, self-styled followers of Christ have perpetrated gruesome acts of violence under the sign of the cross. Over the centuries, the seasons of Lent and Holy Week were a time of fear and trepidation for Jews; Christians have perpetrated some of the worst pogroms as they have remembered the crucifixion of Christ, for which they blamed the Jews. Muslims too associate the cross with violence; crusaders' rampages took place under its sign.

However, an unbiased reading of the story of Jesus Christ gives no warrant for such perpetration of violence. The account of his death in 1 Peter sums up the witness of the whole New Testament well:

> For to this you have been called, because Christ also suffered for you, leaving you an example, so that you should follow in his steps. "He committed no sin, and no deceit was found in his mouth." When he was abused, he did not return abuse; when he suffered, he did not threaten; but he entrusted himself to the one who judges justly. He himself bore our sins in his body on the cross, so that, free from sins, we might live for righteousness. (2:21–24)

If there is a danger in the story of the cross in relation to violence, it is that it might teach mere acquiescence to being mistreated by others, not that it might incite one to abuse. Whenever violence was perpetrated in the name of the cross, the cross was depleted of its "thick" meaning within the larger story of Jesus Christ and "thinned" down to a symbol of religious belonging and power—and the blood of those who did not belong flowed as Christians transmuted themselves from followers of the Crucified to imitators of those who crucified him.

New Creation

Finally, what about the Messiah who is still to come in glory? He will come with grace for his followers. But does not the book of Revelation portray him as a Rider on a white horse whose "eyes are like a flame of fire," whose robe is "dipped in blood," from whose "mouth comes a sharp sword with which to strike down nations," and who is coming to "tread in the wine press of the fury of the wrath of God the Almighty" (19:12–15)? Some New Testament scholars have attempted to reinterpret the Rider so as to make him fit the generally nonviolent stance of the New Testament.[24] What is right about such efforts is that in Revelation the *martyrs* are the true victors, so that, paradoxically, the Beast's victory over them is their victory over the exploitative and violent Beast. In this they mirror Jesus Christ, the slaughtered Lamb, who conquered his enemies precisely by his sacrificial death.[25]

Yet, the Rider is not simply the Lamb; he is the Lamb in his function as *the final judge*. So why is the final judgment necessary? Without it, we would have to presume that all human beings, no matter how deeply steeped in evil they are, will either eventually succumb to the lure of God's love or, if they don't, willingly embrace not only the evil they do but the destructive impact of evil upon their own lives. This belief is not much more than a modern superstition, born out of the inability to look without flinching into the "heart of darkness." First, no doubt, goodness can and does overcome evil. But the power of evil rests in great part in the fact that the more one does evil, the shield that protects one's own evil from being overcome by good becomes thicker. Second, evil is self-contradictory and, if unchecked, is bound to self-destruct. But evildoers do evil more effectively and are better at being evildoers to the degree that they know how to keep making themselves thrive while wreaking havoc on others. The book of Revelation rightly refuses to assume that all evil will either be overcome by good or

49

self-destruct. It therefore cannot exclude the possibility of divine coercion against persistent and unrepentant evildoers. Those who refuse to be redeemed from violence to love by the means of love will be excluded from the world of love.

How should we understand this possible divine coercion? In the context of the whole Christian faith, it is best described as a symbolic portrayal of the final exclusion of everything that refuses to be redeemed by God's suffering love. Will God in fact exclude some human beings in the end? Not necessarily. I called the divine coercion "possible," for it is predicated on human refusal to be made by God into a loving person and therefore to be admitted into the world of love. Will some people refuse? I hope not—and the Bible along with the best of the Christian tradition has never affirmed with certainty that some will refuse and therefore be excluded.[26]

It is possible (though not necessary) that the coming of the new creation will require divine exclusion of what is contrary to the world of perfect love. The crucial question for our purposes is whether this possible divine coercion at the end of history sanctions actual human violence in the middle of it. The response that resounds throughout the New Testament, including the book of Revelation, is a loud and persistent no! Though imitating God is the height of human holiness, there are things that only God may do. One of them is to deploy violence.

Christians are manifestly not to gather under the banner of the Rider on the white horse but to take up their crosses and follow the Crucified. If they were to do otherwise, once again, they would be "thinning" out a "thick" dimension of faith and making a ruinously mischievous use of it. In what way? First, they would illicitly arrogate for themselves what is reserved for God. Second, they would mistakenly transpose the violence from the end time to a time in which God explicitly refrains from deploying violence in order to make repentance possible.

Finally, they would wrongly transmute a future possibility of violence into a present actuality. "Thick" reading of Christian eschatological convictions will not sanction human violence in the present; to the contrary, it will resist it.[27]

In sum, let me underscore one more time that my point in this chapter is not that the Christian faith has not been used to legitimize violence, or that there are no elements in the Christian faith on which such uses build. It is rather that neither the character of the Christian faith (as a monotheistic religion) nor some of its most fundamental convictions (such as that God created the world and is engaged in redeeming it) are violence-inducing. The Christian faith is *misused* when it is employed to underwrite violence.

How does such misuse happen, and how should we prevent it? If we strip Christian convictions of their original and historic cognitive and moral content and reduce faith to a cultural resource endowed with a diffuse aura of the sacred, in situations of conflict we are likely to get religiously legitimized and inspired violence. If we nurture people in historic Christian convictions that are rooted in its sacred texts, we will likely get militants for peace. This, I think, is a result not only of a careful examination of the inner logic of Christian convictions; it is also born by a careful look at actual Christian practice. As R. Scott Appleby has argued on the basis of case studies in *The Ambivalence of the Sacred*, contrary to a widespread misconception, religious people play a positive role in the world of human conflicts and contribute to peace not when they "moderate their religion or marginalize their deeply held, vividly symbolized, and often highly particular beliefs," but rather "when they remain religious actors."[28]

In Place of a Conclusion

If Christian faith is not inherently violent, and if Christians who take their faith seriously are not likely to perpetrate violence, why do misconceptions about the violent character of the Christian faith abound? I have already given part of the answer: Christians have used and continue to use their faith to legitimize violence they deem necessary, and they have done so on a massive scale. Misconceptions of the Christian faith mirror the widespread misbehavior of Christians; and the misbehavior of Christians is associated with misconstruals of their own faith, with the "thinning" out of its "thick" and original elements.[29] But there is more. For one can easily show that the majority of Christians (and the majority of religious folks in general) are nonviolent citizens, peace lovers, peacemakers, some even peace activists—and are such precisely out of religious reasons. The purveyors of violence who seek religious legitimation are statistically a small minority among Christians (as they are among other religions as well).

So why is the contrary opinion widespread? Reasons are many. What Avishai Margalit writes about ethnic belonging applies equally well to religion. "It takes one cockroach found in your food to turn the most otherwise delicious meal into a bad experience. . . . It takes 30 to 40 ethnic groups who are fighting one another to make the 1,500 or more significant ethnic groups in the world who live more or less peacefully look bad."[30] One might describe this as the *self-inflation of the negative*, the tendency of the evil to loom larger than the comparatively much more prevalent good.

This general tendency is strengthened in a modern world whose information flows are pervasively dominated by mass media. Consider the following contrast. A paramilitary who rapes Muslim women with a cross around his neck has made it into the headlines and is immortalized in books on religious violence. Katarina Kruhonja, a medical doctor from Osijek, Croatia, and a recipient of the "Right Livelihood Award" (the alternative Nobel Prize) for her peace initiatives, remains relatively unknown—not to mention the motivation for her work, which is thoroughly religious. She writes that she became a peace activist when, during the Serbian shelling of Osijek, the re-centering of her own self on the crucified Christ "freed [her] will" and "she was able to resist the power of exclusion and the logic of war."[31] We know little about people like Ms. Kruhonja partly because the success of their work demands low visibility. But our unawareness of them also stems from the character of mass-media communication in a market-driven world. Violence sells, so viewers get to see violence, without media outlets being much bothered about a disproportion between represented and actual violence.

The mass media create reality, but they do so by building on the proclivities of viewers. Why does the Serbian paramilitary rapist seem more "interesting" than Ms. Kruhonja? And why are we prone to conclude from the cross he is wearing around his neck that his religious faith is implicated in the acts, whereas it would never occur to us to conclude from the ring on his finger that the institution of marriage is to blame? Religion is more associated with violence than with peace in the public imagination partly because the public is fascinated with violence. We, the peace-loving citizens of nations whose tranquility is secured by effective policing, are insatiable observers of violence. And as voyeurs, we show ourselves as vicarious participants in the very violence we outwardly abhor.[32] We are particularly drawn to religious violence because we have, understandably, a strong interest in exposing hypocrisy, especially of a religious kind. Put the two factors together—inner deployment of violence and delight in exposure—and it looks like we want to hear of religious people's involvement in violence partly because we ourselves are violent but expect them to act otherwise.

If we were more self-critical about our own hidden violent proclivities and more suspicious about the presentation of violence in media, we might observe on the religious landscape not just eruptions of violence but a widespread and steady flow of work that religious people do to make our world into a more peaceful place. Our imagination would then not be captured, for instance, with religion as the motivating force for the not-particularly-religiously-zealous terrorists who destroyed the Twin Towers. Instead, we would be impressed with the degree to which religion served as a source of solace and orientation for the majority of Americans in a time of crisis, with the motivation it gave to many of them to help the victims, to protect Muslims from stereotyping, and to build bridges between religious cultures estranged on account of violence that was triggered largely by nonreligious motives. It is these anonymous people who acted out of the true spirit of Christian faith.

Properly understood, the Christian faith is neither coercive nor idle. As a prophetic religion, Christian faith will be an active faith, engaged in the world in a noncoercive way—offering blessing to our endeavors, effective comfort in our failures, moral guidance in a complex world, and a framework of meaning for our lives and our activities. To be engaged in the world well, Christians will have to keep one thing at the forefront of their attention: the relationship between God and a vision of human flourishing.

4

———————————————————————————————————

Human Flourishing

ope, in a Christian sense, is love stretching itself into
the future.

When I hope, I expect something from the future. But I don't
hope for everything I expect. Some anticipated things—like a
visit to the dentist—I face with dread rather than welcoming
them in hope. "I speak of 'hope,'" wrote Josef Pieper in his
Hope and History, "only when what I am expecting is, in my
view, *good*."[1] And yet, even all good things that come my way
are not a matter of hope. I don't hope for a new day to dawn
after a dark and restful night; I *know*, more or less, that the
sun will rise. But I may hope for cool breezes to freshen up a
hot summer day. In our everyday usage, "hope" is, roughly, the
*expectation of good things that don't come to us as a matter
of course.*

Christian faith adds another layer to this everyday usage
of "hope." In *Theology of Hope* Jürgen Moltmann famously
distinguishes between hope and optimism. Both have to do
with positive expectation, and yet the two are very different.

Optimism has to do with good things in the future that are latent in the past and the present; the future associated with optimism—Moltmann calls it *futurum*—is an unfolding of what is already there. We survey the past and the present, extrapolate about what is likely to happen in the future, and, if the prospects are good, become optimistic. Hope, on the other hand, has to do with good things in the future that come to us from "outside," from God; the future associated with hope—Moltmann calls it *adventus*—is a gift of something new.[2] We hear the word of divine promise, and because God is love we trust in God's faithfulness. God then brings about "a new thing": aged Sarah, barren of womb, gives birth to a son (Gen. 21:1–2; Rom. 4:18–21); the crucified Jesus Christ is raised from the dead (Acts 2:22–36); a mighty Babylon falls and a new Jerusalem comes down from heaven (Rev. 18:1–24; 21:1–5); more generally, the good that seemed impossible becomes not just possible but real.

The expectation of good things that come as a gift from God—that is hope. And that is love too, projecting itself into our and our world's future. For love always gives gifts and is itself a gift; inversely, every genuine gift is an expression of love. At the heart of the hoped-for future, which comes from the God of love, is the flourishing of individuals, communities, and our whole globe. But how is the God of love, "who gives life to the dead and calls into existence things that do not exist" (Rom. 4:17), related to human flourishing? And how should we understand human flourishing if it is a gift of the God of love?

Human Flourishing

Consider with me a prevalent contemporary Western understanding of human flourishing, how it differs from some previous understandings, and what its consequences are.

Satisfaction

Many people in the West today have come to believe—"to feel in their gut" might be a colloquial but more accurate way of putting it—that a flourishing human life is an experientially satisfying human life. By this they don't mean only that the experience of satisfaction is a desirable aspect of human flourishing, so that, all other things being equal, people who experience satisfaction flourish in a more complete way than people who do not. We flourish more, for instance, when we are energetic and healthy than when we are enveloped in sadness and wracked with pain (even if it may be true that pain can be a servant of the good and exhilaration can be deceptive). Though some ancient Stoics believed that one can flourish equally well on the torture rack as in the comfort of one's home, most people from all periods of human history have thought that experiencing satisfaction enhances flourishing.

In contrast, for many in the West, experiential satisfaction is what their lives are all about. It does not merely enhance flourishing; it defines it. Such people cannot imagine themselves as flourishing if they do not experience satisfaction, if they don't *feel happy*, as the preferred way of expressing it goes. For them, flourishing *consists* in having an experientially satisfying life. No satisfaction, no flourishing. Sources of satisfaction may vary, ranging from appreciation of classical music to the use of drugs, from the delights of haute cuisine to sadomasochistic sex, from sports to religion. What matters is not the source of satisfaction but the fact of it. What justifies a given lifestyle or activity is the satisfaction it generates—the pleasure. And when they experience satisfaction, people feel that they flourish.

As Philip Rieff noted in *The Triumph of the Therapeutic* some decades ago (1966), ours is a culture of managed pursuit of pleasure, not a culture of sustained endeavor to lead the good life, as defined by foundational symbols and convictions.[3] This is a broad generalization with many important exceptions. Yet it describes well a major and growing trend.

Love of God and Universal Solidarity

We can contrast contemporary Western culture and its implicit default account of human flourishing with the two dominant models in the history of the Western tradition. Fifth-century church father Augustine, one of the most influential figures in Western religion and culture, represents well the first of these two accounts. In his reflections on the happy life in his major work *On the Trinity*, he writes, "God is the only source to be found of any good things, but especially of those which make a man good and those which will make him happy; only from him do they come into a man and attach themselves to a man."[4] Consequently, human beings flourish and are truly happy when they center their lives on God, the source of everything that is true, good, and beautiful. As to all created things, they too ought to be loved. But the only way to properly love them and fully and truly enjoy them is to love and enjoy them "in God."

Now, Augustine readily agrees with what most people think, namely that those are happy who have everything they want. But he adds immediately that this is true only if they want "nothing wrongly,"[5] which is to say, if they want everything in accordance with the character and will of their Creator, whose very being is love. The supreme good that makes human beings truly happy—in my terminology, the proper content of a flourishing life—consists in love of God and neighbor and enjoyment of both. In his *City of God*, Augustine defines it as a "completely harmonious fellowship in the enjoyment of God, and each other in God."[6]

Around the eighteenth century, a different account of human flourishing emerged in the West. It was connected with what scholars sometimes describe as an "anthropocentric shift"—the gradual redirection of interest from the transcendent God to human beings and their mundane affairs. The new humanism that was born was different "from most ancient ethics of human nature," writes Charles Taylor in *A Secular Age*, in that its notion of human flourishing "makes no reference to something higher which humans should reverence or love or acknowledge."[7] For Augustine and the tradition that followed him, this "something higher" was God. Modern humanism became exclusive by shedding the idea of human lives centered on God.

And yet, even as the new humanism rejected God and the command to love God, it retained the moral obligation to love neighbor. The central pillar of its vision of the good life was a universal beneficence transcending all boundaries of tribe or nation and extending to all human beings. True, this was an ideal that could not be immediately realized (and from which some groups, deemed inferior, were de facto exempt). But the goal toward which humanity was moving with a steady step was a state of human relations in which the flourishing of each was tied to the flourishing of all and the flourishing of all tied to the flourishing of each. Marx's vision of a communist society, encapsulated in the phrase "from each according to his abilities, to each according to his need,"[8] was historically the most influential (and most problematic) version of this idea of human flourishing.

In the late twentieth century another shift occurred. Human flourishing came increasingly to be defined as experiential satisfaction (though, of course, other accounts of human flourishing remain robust as well, whether they derive from religious or secular interpretations of the world). Having lost earlier reference to "something higher which humans should reverence or love," it now lost reference to universal solidarity as well. What remained was concern for the self and the desire for the experience of satisfaction. It is not, of course, that individuals today simply seek pleasure on their own, isolated from society. It is also not that they don't care for others. Others are very much involved. But they matter mainly in that they serve an individual's experience of satisfaction. For religious people in this category, this applies to God no less than to human beings. Desire—the outer shell of love—has remained, but love itself, by being directed exclusively to the self, is lost.

Hope

One way to view the three phases in the conception of human flourishing—love of God and neighbor, universal beneficence, experiential satisfaction—is to see them as a history of the diminution of the object of love: from the vast expanse of the infinite God, love first tapered to the boundaries of the universal human community, and then radically contracted to the narrowness of a single self—one's own self. A parallel contraction has also occurred with the scope of human hope.

In the book *The Real American Dream*, written at the turn of the millennium, Andrew Delbanco traces the diminution of American hope. I am interested in it here because America may be symptomatic in this regard: it would be possible to trace an analogous diminution of hope in most societies that are highly integrated into globalization processes. A glance at the book's table of contents reveals the main point of his analysis. The chapter headings read: "God," "Nation," "Self." The infinite God and the eternal life of enjoying God and one's neighbors (at least some of them!) was the hope of the Puritans who founded America. American nationalists of the nineteenth century, notably Abraham Lincoln, transformed this Christian imagery, in which God was at the center, into "the symbol of a redeemer nation." In the process, they created a "new symbol of hope."[9] The scope of hope was significantly reduced,[10] and yet there still remained something of immense importance to hope for—the prospering of the nation which itself was a "chosen people," called upon to "bear the ark of the Liberties of the world," as Melville put it.[11] But then, in the aftermath of the 1960s and 1980s, as a result of the combined hippy and yuppie revolutions, "instant gratification" became "the hallmark of the good life." It is only a minor exaggeration to say that hope was reduced "to the scale of self-pampering."[12] Moving from the vastness of God down to the ideal of a redeemer nation, hope has narrowed, argues Delbanco, "to the vanishing point of the self alone."[13]

Earlier on I noted that when the scope of love diminishes, love itself disappears; benevolence and beneficence mutate into the pursuit of self-interest. Something similar happens to hope, which is understandable if hope is love stretching itself into the future of the beloved object, as I have suggested at the beginning of this chapter. So when love shrinks to self-interest, and self-interest devolves into the experience of satisfaction, hope disappears as well. As Michael Oakeshott rightly insists, hope depends on finding some "end to be pursued more extensive than a merely instant desire."[14]

Unsatisfying Satisfaction

Love and hope are not the only casualties when the experience of satisfaction becomes the center of human striving. As many have pointed out, satisfaction itself is threatened by the pursuit of pleasure. I don't mean simply that we spend a good deal of our lives dissatisfied. Clearly, we are dissatisfied until we experience satisfaction. Desire is aroused, and striving begins, goaded by a sense of discontentment and pulled by the expectation of fulfillment until satisfaction is reached. Dissatisfied and expectant striving is the overall state, and fulfillment is its interruption; desire is eternal, and satisfaction is fleetingly periodic.[15]

More important, almost paradoxically, we remain dissatisfied in the midst of experiencing satisfaction. We compare our "pleasures" to those of others and begin to envy them. The fine new Honda of our modest dreams is a source of *dissatisfaction* when we see a neighbor's new Mercedes. But even when we win the game of comparisons—when we park in front of our garage the best model of the most expensive car—our victory is hollow, melancholy. As Gratiano puts it in Shakespeare's *Merchant of Venice*, "All things that are, are with more spirit chased than enjoyed."[16] First, marked as we are by what philosophers call self-transcendence, in our imagination we are always already beyond any state we have reached. Whatever we have, we want more and different things, and when we have climbed to the top, a sense of disappointment clouds the triumph. Our striving can therefore find proper rest only when we find joy in something infinite. For Christians, this something is God.

Second, we feel melancholy because our pleasure is truly human and therefore truly pleasurable only if it has meaning beyond itself. So it is with sex, for instance. No matter how enticing and thrilling it may be, it leaves an aftertaste of dissatisfaction—maybe guilt, but certainly emptiness—if it does not somehow refer beyond itself, if it is not a sacrament of love between human beings. It is similar with many other pleasures.[17]

When we place pleasure at the center of the good life, when we decouple it from the love of God, the ultimate source of meaning, and when we sever it from love of neighbor and hope for a common future, we are left, in the words of Andrew Delbanco, "with no way of organizing desire into a structure of meaning."[18] And for meaning-making animals as we humans ineradicably are, such desire to satisfy self-contained pleasures will always remain deeply unsatisfying.

Accounts of Reality, Conceptions of Flourishing

For the sake of the fulfillment of individuals, of the thriving of communities, and of our common global future, we need a better account of human flourishing than experiential satisfaction. The most robust alternative visions of human flourishing are embodied in the great faith traditions. It is to them—and the debates between them as to what human flourishing truly consists in—that we need to turn for resources to think anew about human flourishing. In what follows, I will suggest contours of a vision of human flourishing as contained in the Christian faith (or rather, one strand of that faith). A vision of human flourishing—and resources to realize it—is the most important contribution of the Christian faith to the common good.

The Centrality of Human Flourishing

Concern with human flourishing is at the heart of the great faiths, including Christianity. True, you cannot always tell that from the way faiths are practiced. When surveying their history, it seems on occasion as if their goals were simply to dispatch people out of this world and into the next—out of the veil of tears into heavenly bliss (Christianity), or out of the world of craving into nirvana (Buddhism), to give just two examples. And yet, for great religious teachers, even for the representatives of highly ascetical and seemingly otherworldly forms of faith, human flourishing has always remained central.

Take Abu Hamid Muhammad al-Ghazali, one of the greatest Islamic thinkers, as an example. "Know, O beloved, that man was not created in jest or at random, but marvelously made and for some great end," he begins one of his books. What is that great end for a being whose spirit is "lofty and divine," even if its body is "mean and earthly"? Here is how al-Ghazali describes it:

> When in the crucible of abstinence he [man] is purged from
> carnal passions he attains to the highest, and in place of being
> a slave to lust and anger becomes endued with angelic qualities.
> Attaining that state, he finds his heaven in the contemplation of
> Eternal Beauty, and no longer in fleshly delights.

These lines come from the introduction to al-Ghazali's book,
which is all about "turning away from the world to God." That
may make it sound as if the book is not about human flourishing
at all. And yet its title is *The Alchemy of Happiness*.[19] Precisely
by talking about turning away from the world to God and purg-
ing oneself from carnal passions, the book *is* about flourishing,
in this world and the next.

Or take one of the greatest Jewish thinkers, Moses Maimonides. At the beginning of *The Guide of the Perplexed*, he
writes that the image of God in human beings—that which distinguishes them from animals—is "the intellect which God made
overflow into man."[20] To underscore this point, Maimonides
ends his work by stating that intellect is "the bond between us
and Him."[21] True human perfection consists

> in the acquisition of the rational virtues—I refer to the con-
> ception of intelligibles, which teach true opinions concerning
> divine things. This is in true reality the ultimate end; this is what
> gives the individual true perfection, a perfection belonging to
> him alone; and it gives him permanent perdurance; through it
> man is man.[22]

The nature of ultimate reality, the character of human beings,
the meaning of their lives, and the most worthy of their pur-
suits—all these things cohere. The whole religious system is
connected with human flourishing.

Contemporary fellow Muslims and Jews might quarrel with
al-Ghazali's and Maimonides's accounts of human flourishing,
most likely deeming them too ascetical or intellectual. Indeed

64

many internal debates within a religious tradition concern the question of just what it is that constitutes properly understood human flourishing. Christians might do so as well (though many Christian sages and saints have understood flourishing in strikingly similar ways).[23] Christians might also disagree about the best means to achieve it (noting especially the absence of Jesus Christ in these accounts). My point in invoking al-Ghazali and Maimonides is not to offer a Christian assessment of their thought, though a respectful critical conversation among great faiths about human flourishing is important. It is rather to illustrate that the concern for human flourishing is central to great religious traditions, one of their defining characteristics.

Not so long ago human flourishing was also central to the institutions of higher learning in the West. They were largely about exploration of what it means to live well, to lead a meaningful life. They were less about how to be successful at this or that activity or vocation but about how to be successful *at being human*. In my terms, they were about human flourishing. This is no longer so. In *Education's End* Anthony Kronman tells a compelling story of how the ideal of a "research university" and fascination with "postmodernism" in culture and theory colluded in making colleges and universities give up on exploring the meaning of life.[24] Today, he writes, "if one wants organized assistance in answering the question of life's meaning, and not just the love of family and friends, it is to the churches that one must turn."[25]

As a self-confessed secularist, Kronman is critical of the way religious traditions go about giving answer to the meaning of life. He believes—wrongly, I think—that faiths are inherently inhospitable to responsible pluralism and always demand a sacrifice of intellect. As a person of faith, I think that a secular quest for the meaning of life is very likely to fail, and that the viable candidates for the meaning of life are all religiously based.

But whatever position one takes in the debate between secular humanism and religious traditions, both share a concern for human flourishing and stand in contrast with a pervasive cultural preoccupation with experiential satisfaction in wide swaths of societies today, in the West and elsewhere.

Fit

Al-Ghazali's *The Alchemy of Happiness* and Maimonides's *The Guide of the Perplexed* not only illustrate the centrality of human flourishing to religious traditions; they also highlight one significant way in which religious accounts of human flourishing differ from the contemporary propensity to see flourishing as experiential satisfaction. The difference concerns a fit between how the world, including human beings, is constituted and what it means for human beings to flourish. The central chapters of al-Ghazali's book, for instance, deal with the knowledge of the self, of God, of this world, and of the next world.[26] To know what it means to reach happiness, you need to know who you are and what your place is in the larger household of reality—created and uncreated.

In this regard, al-Ghazali is not unusual. As illustrated by Maimonides, most religions and most significant philosophies operate with the idea that there is a fit—maybe a loose fit, but some kind of fit nonetheless—between an overarching account of reality and a proper conception of human flourishing. And most people in most places throughout human history have agreed that there should be such a fit. They have done so mainly because their lives were guided by religious traditions. Let me flesh out this notion of a fit by stepping away for a moment from religious figures such as Augustine and al-Ghazali and looking briefly at two philosophers, one ancient and one modern: Seneca and Nietzsche.

Seneca and the ancient Stoics (who have benefitted from something of a comeback in recent years)[27] coordinated their convictions about the world, about human beings, about what it means to live well, and about the nature of happiness.[28] They believed that god is Cosmic Reason, spread throughout creation and directing its development completely. Human beings are primarily rational creatures; they live well when they align themselves with Cosmic Reason. They are happy when, in alignment with Cosmic Reason, they achieve tranquil self-sufficiency and are not subject to emotions such as fear, envy, or anger, no matter what the outward circumstances might be. Thus, Stoic accounts of the world and of human flourishing cohere.

My second example, Friedrich Nietzsche, was a modern thinker radically opposed not just to Christianity but also to the ancient Stoics.[29] Even he, an antirealist thinker suspicious of all systems, seems not to have been able to shake off the idea of a fit between an intellectually responsible understanding of the world and what it means for human beings to flourish within that world. The whole Western tradition of morality should be rejected, he believed, not just because it is to blame if "man, as a species, never reach[es] his highest potential power and splendor."[30] The Western tradition of morality is inappropriate primarily because it does not fit who human beings actually are. Contrary to the assumptions of Western moral traditions, human beings are (1) not free in their actions but governed by necessity; (2) not transparent to themselves and others in their motivations, but opaque; (3) not similar to each other and therefore subject to the same moral code, but each different. Conversely, Nietzsche's own advocacy of the "will to power" of "higher humans" fits precisely these features of human beings and makes possible the maximization of the excellence of "higher humans."[31] His "will to power" is simply the tendency of all beings—humans included—not just to survive, but to enlarge and expand—to flourish, so to speak, even at the expense of others. In a way completely different from the Stoics, Nietzsche's account of human flourishing also fits his account of reality as a whole.

Absence of Fit

In contrast, those among our contemporaries who think that flourishing consists in experiential satisfaction tend not to care about how this notion of flourishing fits with the character of the world and of human beings. The reason is not simply that, for the most part, they are ordinary people rather than philosophers (like Seneca or Nietzsche) or great religious thinkers (like Augustine, al-Ghazali, or Maimonides). After all, over the centuries and up to the present, many ordinary people have cared about aligning their lives with the character of the world and of ultimate reality. No, the primary reasons have to do with the nature of the contemporary account of flourishing and the general cultural milieu prevalent in today's Western world.

First, as I have noted already, satisfaction is central in how many contemporaries think of human flourishing. Satisfaction is a form of experience, and experiences are generally deemed to be matters of individual preference. Everyone is the best judge of her own experience of satisfaction. To examine whether a particular experience fits into a larger account of the world is already to risk relativizing its value as an experience.

As an illustration, consider a religious version of the account of human flourishing as experiential satisfaction. In such cases, faith will shed its power to orient people and will be reduced to a servant of experiential satisfaction—which is, as I noted above, a major malfunction of faith. From being revered as the "Creator and the Master of the Universe," who by that very identity defines who human beings are and how they should live, God is then transformed into something like a combination of "Divine Butler" and "Cosmic Therapist."[32] Instead of faith framing and defining experience of satisfaction, experience of satisfaction defines faith.

This sort of transformation of faith is in line with the pervasively antimetaphysical tenor of contemporary Western culture. "In post-Nietzschean spirit," writes Terry Eagleton, "the West appears to be busily undermining its own erstwhile metaphysical foundations with an unholy mélange of practical materialism, political pragmatism, moral and cultural relativism, and philosophical skepticism."[33] In his book *The Meaning of Life*, he notes that many contemporary intellectuals, unsurprisingly, tend to dismiss serious reflection on "human life as a whole as disreputably 'humanist'—or indeed as the kind of 'totalizing' theory which led straight to the death camps of the totalitarian state." In their view, there is "no such thing as humanity or human life to be contemplated";[34] there are only various culturally conditioned and individually inflected changing life projects. If each person is an artist of her own life, aiming to achieve experiential satisfaction unconstrained by moral norms reflective of a common human nature, then it seems superfluous to ask how the stream of ever new artistic self-creations aimed at experiential satisfaction fit within the larger account of reality.

My point is not that it would be impossible to offer a plausible interpretation of reality—"plausible," I write, not "true"!—into which an account of human flourishing as experiential satisfaction could be nestled comfortably. My point is that many today would not care whether they live with or against the grain of reality. They want what they want, and the fact that they want it is a sufficient justification for wanting it. Arguments about how their desires fit with a more encompassing account of reality—how they relate to "human nature," for instance—are simply beside the point.

Creator and Creatures

It is a mistake—a major mistake—not to worry about how well our notion of flourishing fits the nature of reality. If we live against the grain of reality, we will experience emotional highs, but we will not find lasting satisfaction, let alone be able to live fulfilled lives. That's what the Christian tradition, along with other great religious and philosophical traditions, has always insisted. The great Christian saints, theologians, and lay leaders of the past believed that accounts of human flourishing had to cohere with ideas about God as the source and goal of all reality. But how should they be made to cohere?

At the very outset, we can eliminate one possible option. We cannot start with a preferred account of human flourishing and then construct a picture of God to go with it, designing the fit between God and human flourishing the way we might look for a jacket to match our slacks. We would then be consciously enacting Nietzsche's devastating critique of the emergence of Christian morality and Christian faith as a whole. According to Nietzsche, Christians designed false beliefs about God in order to legitimize their preferred values. If we were to start with an idea of human flourishing and then "build" God to match our values, then the only difference between Nietzsche's version and ours would be Nietzsche's dismissal of those values as being perverse, as opposed to our upholding of them as healthy. More important, by constructing a picture of God so as to fit already given notions of human flourishing, we would be enacting one of the most troubling malfunctions of faith—divesting faith of its own integrity and making it simply an instrument of our own interests and purposes.

Let's return once more to Augustine. We may sum up his convictions about God, the world, human beings, and human flourishing in four brief propositions, tailored to highlight the relation of his position to that of the Stoics, Nietzsche, and many of our contemporaries. First, he believed that God is not an impersonal Reason dispersed throughout the world but a "person" who loves and can be loved in return. Second, to be human is to love; we can chose *what* to love but not *whether* to love. Third, we live well when we love both God and neighbor, aligning ourselves with the God who loves. Fourth, we will flourish and be truly happy when we discover joy in loving the infinite God and our neighbors in God.

For Augustine, convictions about God, human beings, and human flourishing all cohere. That's the positive side of the fit: it specifies what is "in," so to speak, when it comes to human flourishing. But the fit also specifies what is "out." If we share Augustine's convictions about God and human beings, we have to reject some interpretations of reality and some accounts of human flourishing. Consider once again, now from an Augustinian perspective, the Stoic, Nietzschean, and contemporary Western accounts of flourishing.

If we believe that God is love and that we are created for love, the Stoic ideal of tranquil self-sufficiency will not do. Instead of caring for our neighbor's well-being to the extent that we care about leading our lives well, as the Stoics did, we will care for our neighbor's well-being—including their tranquility—for their own sake, not just ours.[35] Our concern will then be not just to lead life well ourselves. Instead, we will strive for life to go well for our neighbors and for them to lead their lives well, and we will acknowledge that their flourishing is tied deeply to our flourishing.[36]

Similarly, if we believe that God is love and that we are created for love, we will be disinclined to believe that the Nietzschean noble morality designed to further the excellence of the "higher humans" is a proper road to human flourishing. Compassion and help for those whose lives do not go well—for the vulnerable, the weak—will then be an essential component of leading *our* lives well.

71

Finally, if we believe that God is love and that we are created for love, we will reject the notion that flourishing consists in being experientially satisfied. Instead, we will believe that we will be experientially satisfied when we truly flourish. When is it that we truly flourish? When is it that we lead our lives well, and our lives are going well? We lead our lives well when we love God with our whole being and when we love our neighbors as we (properly) love ourselves. Life goes well for us when our basic needs are met and when we experience that we are loved by God and by our neighbors—when we are loved as who we are, with our own specific character and history, notwithstanding our fragility and failures. Echoing Augustine's comment on the contrast between Epicurean and Christian visions of happiness, instead of our slogan being, "Let us eat and drink" (or some more sophisticated version of the same that privileges "higher pleasures"), it should be, "Let us give and pray."[37]

Loving God, Loving Neighbor

What I have written about the relation between God and human flourishing is but a theological echo of two central verses from the Christian Scriptures: "God is love" (1 John 4:8) and "You shall love the Lord your God with all your heart, and with all your soul, and with all your strength, and with all your mind; and your neighbor as yourself" (Luke 10:27). Each of these verses, in a different way and with a specific Christian inflection, repeats themes deeply rooted in the Hebrew Scriptures—themes of God's abiding love for Israel (Exod. 34:6) and God's command to love God and neighbor (Lev. 19:18; Deut. 6:5). In conclusion, let me apply this notion of human flourishing, together with its undergirding convictions about God, to the proper functions of faith in human life.

As I note in chapter 1, every prophetic religion, including the Christian faith, has the following two fundamental movements: the ascent to God to receive the prophetic message, and the return to the world to bring the received message to bear on mundane realities. Both movements are essential. Without ascent, there is nothing to impart; without return, there is no one to impart to.

Most malfunctions of faith are rooted in a failure to love the God of love or a failure to love the neighbor. Ascent malfunctions happen when we don't love God as we should. We either love our interests, purposes, and projects, and then employ language about God to realize them (we may call this "functional reduction"), or we love the wrong God (we may call this "idolatric substitution"). Return malfunctions happen when we love neither our neighbor nor ourselves properly—when faith either merely energizes or heals us but does not shape our lives so that we live them to our own and our neighbors' benefit, or when we impose our faith on our neighbors irrespective of their wishes.

The challenge facing Christians is ultimately very simple: love God and neighbor rightly so that we may both avoid malfunctions of faith and relate God positively to human flourishing. And yet, the challenge is also complex and difficult. Let me highlight three aspects.

First, we need to *explicate* God's relation to human flourishing with regard to many concrete issues we are facing today—from poverty to environmental degradation, from bioethical issues to international relations, from sex to governing. Without showing how a Christian understanding of God and vision of human flourishing apply to concrete issues, these notions will remain vague and inert, with little impact on the way we actually live.

Second, we need to *make plausible* the claim that the love of God and of neighbor is the key to human flourishing. For centuries, nonbelievers have not just called into question God's existence but have railed against God's nature, against the way God relates to the world, and consequently against theistic accounts of how humans ought to live in relation to God. Sometimes it feels as if they would not have minded God existing if they could have just believed that God is good for us. And this just underscores how difficult it is to make plausible to nonbelievers the connection between God and human flourishing. For the notion of what is "good for us"—and not just the existence and character of God—is highly contested.

Third, maybe the most difficult challenge for Christians is to actually *believe* that God is fundamental to human flourishing. Now, it is not sufficient for us to believe it as we might believe that there may be water on some distant planet. We must believe it as a rock-bottom conviction that shapes the way we think, preach, write, and live. Charles Taylor tells the story of hearing Mother Theresa speak about her motivation for working with the abandoned and the dying of Calcutta. She explained that she did the hard work of tending them because they were created in the image of God. Being a Catholic philosopher, Taylor thought to himself, "I could have said that too!" And then, being an introspective person and a fine philosopher, he asked himself, "But could I have *meant* it?"

That, I think, is today's most fundamental challenge for theologians, priests and ministers, and Christian laypeople: to *really mean* that the presence and activity of the God of love, who can make us love our neighbors as ourselves, is our hope and the hope of the world—that this God is the secret of our flourishing as persons, cultures, and interdependent inhabitants of a single globe.

PART II

ENGAGED FAITH

5

Identity and Difference

One Player among Many

Religions, especially Christianity, are thriving in many parts of the world today. At the same time, a sense of crisis has gripped many Christian communities in the West. Once they were dominant social institutions in what was deemed to be "the Christian West"; today they find themselves increasingly on the margins, in some places even in exile. Much like skyscrapers have dwarfed churches (some of which, like Dowanhill Church in Glasgow, have been remodeled into theaters, lecture halls, bars, restaurants, and even nightclubs), other important religious and nonreligious social players have sidelined Christian communities. Western churches have a past they like to boast about but a future they seem to dread.

Not willing to embrace this new diminished role, some Christian communities still try to insert themselves as contenders in the major league social games. More often than not, however, they find out that few of their old tricks work anymore; they trip over the ball and don't know how to pass, let alone how to score. The history of the Christian Right in the United States, from the 1970s to the present, could be seen as a story of the failed attempts of some Christian communities to regain their erstwhile influence through political means.

It is understandable that Christians seek social influence. Responsibility to "mend the world" and serve the common good is inscribed into the very character of Christianity as a prophetic religion; it is a consequence of the commitment to love both the one God and neighbors. But in the future, Christians will likely exert that influence less from the centers of power and more from social margins. Moreover, whether they find themselves close to the centers or far from them, in a religiously and culturally pluralistic world, Christian communities will be only one of many players.

For those familiar with the early history of the Christian church—and for careful observers of young and vibrant Christian communities in the non-Western world—there is something odd about the present sense of crisis in the West. The early Christian communities were not major social players at all! They were not even among the cheering or booing spectators. Slandered, discriminated against, and even persecuted minorities, they were at most a bit of a thorn in society's flesh. Yet, notwithstanding their marginality, early Christian communities celebrated hope in God and proclaimed joyfully the resurrected Lord as they endeavored to walk in the footsteps of the crucified Messiah. It was he who taught them,

> Blessed are those who are persecuted for righteousness' sake, for theirs is the kingdom of heaven. Blessed are you when people revile you and persecute you and utter all kinds of evil things against you falsely on my account. Rejoice and be glad, for your reward is great in heaven, for in the same way they persecuted the prophets who were before you. (Matt. 5:10–11)

For the early Christian communities, to be persecuted was not a cause of alarm but an (unpleasant) occasion for rejoicing. To be tucked in a dark corner outside the public view was not a sign of failure but of keeping good company. Much like many persecuted followers of Christ in the world today, the early churches seemed to have dealt with their precarious marginality with confidence and creativity. We in the West, in contrast, are already alarmed about diminished influence. In the midst of fierce opposition, early Christians celebrated and embodied a way of life—life that they experienced as God's gift and that was modeled on Christ, a paragon of true humanity. In contrast, living in freedom and economic prosperity, many churches in the West, primarily in the United States, bemoan the loss of influence and scheme how to regain it by acquiring political power.

I will forgo here peering into the past to trace the developments that brought Western churches to where they are today—both to their robust sense of social responsibility and to the expectation to be a dominant or at least important force in public life. Instead, I will turn toward the future and try to reimagine the relation between the gospel and the multiple religious and nonreligious cultures in contemporary societies. My goal is to dispel the gloom and generate new hope for Christian communities at the beginning of the twenty-first century—both a more modest and a more robust hope than the churches in the West have had in recent times. To state my goal pointedly: I want to make Christian communities more comfortable with being just one of many players, so that from whatever place they find themselves—on the margins, at the center, or anywhere in between—they can promote human flourishing and the common good.[1] Under different circumstances, they may then reacquire the vibrancy and confidence of the early churches.

The outline of this chapter is simple. First, I note four major features of contemporary societies and the kinds of relations between Christian communities and the wider culture these features do or do not favor. Second, I briefly explore what I consider to be three inadequate ways to live as Christians in these societies. Third, I propose a better way.

Social Context

Four features of contemporary societies provide the framework for how Christian communities should understand their identity in today's world and how they should promote human flourishing and the common good. To sketch the four features as they impact Christian communities, I will build on the famous contrast between "church" and "sect," which Max Weber and Ernst Troeltsch drew more than a century ago.

Voluntarism

According to Weber's distinction between "church" and "sect," a person is born into a church but voluntarily joins a sect.[2] The "church" is more like a family, while the "sect" is more like a club; you are born into one, but you choose to join the other. In contemporary societies, only "sects" exist, more or less. Rather than being assigned to religious communities irrespective of our will, we mostly choose them.[3] Granted, Christian communities are held together by more than just the choices of their members. We get attached to certain people, places, and rituals; we get habituated into certain ecclesiastical practices. And yet in all of this our choices play an indispensable role; we can always leave and join another group.[4] Even if it is true that choices are shaped by many factors,[5] all religious communities live through the choices of their members.

80

Difference

According to Weber's contrast between "church" and "sect," all who are born into the church belong to the church; they are its many and diverse sons and daughters, saints and inveterate sinners alike, and everyone in between. In contrast, the "sect" is an association of those who are "religiously and ethically qualified."[6] In contemporary societies, this distinction is watered down. If everybody is choosing to belong and if, correspondingly, groups receive or reject new members, religious communities will be identified by religious affinities that distinguish their members from nonmembers. "Churches," in Weber's sense, acquire the characteristics of "sects."

Christian communities will be able to survive and thrive in contemporary societies only if they attend to their "difference" from surrounding cultures and subcultures. The following principle stands: whoever wants the Christian communities to exist must want their difference from the surrounding culture, not their blending into it. As a consequence, Christian communities must "manage" their identity by actively engaging in "boundary maintenance."[7] Without boundaries, communities dissolve. The question is not whether there should be boundaries; it is rather what their nature should be (i.e., how permeable should they be) and how they should be maintained (i.e., by shoring up that which is specific to Christian communities or by strengthening that which is central).[8]

Pluralism

According to Ernst Troeltsch, who elaborated on Max Weber's ideas about "church" and "sect," "church" affirms the world whereas "sect" opposes it.[9] Though it had the value of a good caricature, it is not clear that this distinction was useful even when Troeltsch originally formulated it.[10] Today it has lost most of its plausibility. The one cultural world, which the "church" could affirm or the "sect" deny, has splintered into a plurality of rapidly changing cultural worlds that exist within overarching national and global frameworks. These cultural worlds are partly compatible and partly incompatible, partly mutually dependent and partly independent. They form partly overlapping spaces and create ever-changing hybrid subcultures. Simple denial or affirmation of such a world is impossible. Similarly, the simple claim that the Christian message is (or can be made) intelligible to "the world" will not do. We need more complex ways of thinking about the relation to culture to take into account the complex and rapidly changing plurality of cultural worlds that makes up contemporary societies.[11]

Relative Self-Sufficiency

According to the typology, the "church" is at the center of society and influential whereas the "sect" is at its margins and socially impotent. "Church" enters into compromises with the world in order to try to shape it in accordance with God's will, whereas "sect" keeps pure—leaving the world to the "prince of darkness" or, rarely, trying to transmute it into the "new Jerusalem"—and remains socially inconsequential.[12]

Today, this distinction is implausible. First, what sociologists call the "functional differentiation" of society—the fact that various social subsystems specialize in performing particular functions, such as economic, educational, or communication activities—implies the (relative) self-sufficiency and self-perpetuation of social subsystems. And that, in turn, means that the subsystems resist being influenced by values that come from outside.[13] Moreover, the most powerful of these subsystems—economic and communication subsystems—are global rather than local in character.

Second, unlike in traditional societies with their chiefs, kings, or dictators, no center of power holds contemporary societies and the global world order as a whole together by controlling and directing their functioning. In many ways in contemporary cultures, nobody is in control (and the world seems out of control[14]). Within certain parameters and ranges of possibilities, rapid cultural change today happens as a result of multiple interactions between diverse players—diverse in interests and values as well as in the degree of power.

The internet may be a paradigmatic case of the "culture" of diminished control. First, the internet has had an immense cultural impact throughout the world, but this cultural impact is a result neither of the intention of its inventors nor of anybody's subsequent control. When J. C. R. Licklider thought of social interaction through a globally interconnected set of computers, I doubt he intended the mushrooming of the pornography industry. Second, although the internet "has been programmed with a set of options built into different interfaces and platforms" and although it is managed with a heavy hand in some countries, still users are "simultaneously consumers and producers," and can "customize and creatively appropriate this space for their own needs and outcomes." In the process, new forms of authority, outside of "normal flows of authority or traditional vetting processes," come in and out of existence.[15] Control is exercised, but it is diffuse; nobody is in control of the whole process.

Like everyone else, Christian communities can exert influence in contemporary societies mainly from within, only in a piecemeal fashion, and without being able to control the results of their engagements. For comprehensive change, a global revolution would be necessary. As a consequence, Christian communities must learn how to work vigorously for the limited change that is possible, to mourn over persistent and seemingly ineradicable evils, and to celebrate the good wherever it happens and whoever its agents are.[16]

Before discussing a better way for Christianity to relate to culture, I first need to examine briefly what I have come to think of as inadequate proposals about how Christian communities should understand their presence in contemporary societies and serve the common good. By critiquing them, I will pave the road for getting at a better way to think about this issue.

The Liberal Program: Accommodation

One way to think about Christian engagement with the broader culture for the common good, associated with classical theological liberalism, runs roughly like this: translate the Christian message into the conceptualities of the culture in which you live, and adjust your values to its social practices. Such accommodation is possible, the argument goes, because the modern convictions and practices either are themselves an outworking of what lies at the core of the Christian faith or are in sync with it. The accommodation is necessary because otherwise the faith would remain tied to the relics from the past—implausible interpretations of reality and outdated moral convictions—and cease to be compelling to people today. From this perspective, the choice is between accommodation and irrelevance.

Yet, as a general strategy rather than a result of ad hoc decisions, accommodation is wrongheaded for at least two reasons. The first has to do with the fast pace of cultural change in contemporary societies. G. K. Chesterton famously quipped that "those who marry the spirit of the age will find themselves widows in the next." Today, all such marriages are bound to be very short-lived. The second has to do with the combined effect of the pluralistic character of contemporary culture and the sense that nobody is in control. The consequence is that Christian communities are accommodating to what they have not shaped and are able to shape only in a limited way. Indeed, by accommodating, they are in effect giving up on promoting change.

Reconstructions of the Christian faith guided by the strategy of accommodation carry in themselves the seeds of possible Christian self-destruction.[17] After they have accommodated, for the most part what remains for Christian communities to do is to appear after a non-Christian show and repeat the performance in their own way for an audience with Christian scruples. The voice of the Christian communities has become a mere echo of a voice that is not their own. With their characteristic hyperbole, Stanley Hauerwas and Will Willimon put the consequence of the accommodation strategy this way: "Alas, in leaning over to speak to the modern world, we had fallen in. We had lost the theological resources to resist, lost the resources even to see that there was something worth resisting."[18]

The Postliberal Program: Reversing the Direction of Conformation

The postliberal alternative is, in a sense, the obverse of the liberal program. Commenting on it, Nicholas Wolterstorff describes its basic thrust as "reversing the direction of conformation."[19] Instead of translating the biblical message into the conceptualities of the culture one inhabits, as liberal theology sought to do, Christians should redescribe the world anew with the help of the biblical story.[20] The whole history of the world—including contemporary societies with their multiple and changing cultures, each with their partly overlapping, partly conflicting sets of beliefs and practices—is situated within the story of God's dealing with creation to redeem it and bring it to its final consummation. Christians should interpret the world and act in it in light of that story.

85

But by inhabiting the biblical story, have the Christian communities not closed themselves off from a meaningful conversation with the larger culture? The advocates of the postliberal program resolutely reject this suggestion. For such conversation to happen, however, two conditions must be met. First, if we think of Christian churches as distinct communities of discourse, as some postliberals do, there must be at least some significant "cultural-linguistic" compatibility between the Christian churches and the non-Christian cultural worlds. Otherwise communication will falter.

Second, conversation with non-Christians presupposes Christian readiness to listen and learn. It would be both arrogant and foolish of Christians to interpret the larger culture merely from their own perspective, not paying attention to how others interpret themselves or how others interpret Christian communities. Wolterstorff asks critically,

> But is the relation of the Church theologian to the non-theological disciplines exclusively that of melting down gold taken from the Egyptians? Isn't some of the statuary of the Egyptians quite OK as it is? Does it all reek of idolatry? Isn't there something for the Church theologian to learn from the non-theological disciplines?[21]

A more complex approach is required than what the metaphor of "reversing the direction of conformation" suggests. We should be able to decide case by case in which direction the conformation ought to go—a stance consonant with some versions of the postliberal position.[22] From what standpoint should the followers of Christ make such ad hoc decisions about the direction of conformation? A neutral one? No such neutral standpoint is available. And in any case, for Christians the governing standpoint is that of God's revelation in Jesus Christ. This is the center that defines the identity of Christian churches—their

86

internal character, their difference from surrounding cultures, and the proper mode of boundary maintenance.[23]

It might seem that the two conditions for Christian conversation with non-Christian cultural worlds call into question the difference of Christian communities from the surrounding culture. Both the partial symbolic compatibility and the readiness to learn require a good deal of proximity. If we take these conditions seriously, what happens to distance, to difference, to boundary maintenance? Do not the dangers of accommodation lurk around the corner?

The Separatist Program: Retreat from the World

One way to avoid the dangers of accommodation is to imagine Christian communities as islands in the sea of worldliness. They would then have their own territory that is as clearly set apart from the wider culture as are the rocks that protrude from the waters. This could be seen as a radical version of the postliberal position.

In *Discipleship*, Dietrich Bonhoeffer describes churches as being "in the midst of the world" but as those who are "taken out of the world."[24] Their environment is "a foreign land" to them. Using a more dynamic image, he thought of Christians as strangers "only passing through the country," and of Christian communities like a "sealed train." He writes,

> At any moment [the Christian community] may receive the signal to move on. Then it will break camp, leaving behind all worldly friends and relatives, and following only the voice of the one who has called it. It leaves the foreign country and moves onward toward its heavenly home.[25]

In penning these words, Bonhoeffer was giving pastoral advice to a church facing the Nazi regime. In an environment of totalitarian cultural madness he saw Christian presence in the world as *passage*—as the wandering on earth of those whose "life lies in heaven."[26] If one isolates such an account of the relation between church and the world from its specific situation and elevates it to a general program for Christian presence in the world, serious problems arise.

If Christian communities only wander on earth but live in heaven, they will have their own truth and their own moral norms, their own practices, all of which would not only be determined exclusively by God's revelation in Jesus Christ but would have little to do with what is considered true, good, and beautiful outside the sealed train in which they live. Christians would then be present in a given culture but would remain completely external to it.

The fundamental theological problem with such an external view of Christian presence in the world is a mistaken understanding of the earthly habitats of Christian communities. It presupposes that the culture in which they live is a foreign country pure and simple, a land bereft of God, rather than a world that God created and pronounced good. If, as a consequence, Christian communities withdraw from the world and turn inward, the result will be the idleness of the Christian faith as a prophetic religion (see chapters 1 and 2). On the other hand, if such Christian communities enter the world and attempt to remake it in their own image—if they become what are sometimes called "aggressive sects"—the Christian faith will become coercive (see chapters 1 and 3). In this case, the relation of Christian communities to culture would be similar to what Qutb advocated with regard to Islam (see the introduction).

Yet it would contradict major Christian convictions to think that the world outside Christian communities is bereft of God's active presence. The God who gives "new birth" is not only the "Father of our Lord Jesus Christ" (1 Pet. 1:3) but also the Creator and sustainer of the world with all its cultural diversity.

As the Word came "to what was his own" (John 1:11) when it dwelled in Jesus Christ, so also Christians live in each culture as in their own proper space. Cultures are not *foreign countries* for the followers of Christ but rather *their own homelands, the creation of the one God*. If Christians are estranged from the world, it can only be because and insofar as the world is (and maybe they themselves as well are) estranged from God. Christian communities should not seek to leave their home cultures and establish settlements outside or live as islands within them. Instead, they should remain in them and change them—subvert the power of the foreign force and seek to bring the culture into closer alignment with God and God's purposes. With the possible exception of when a culture has gone seriously awry—as in Nazi Germany—Christian "difference" should always remain *internal* to a given cultural world.

Internal Difference: A Better Way

How should we understand public engagement if Christian presence is *internal* difference? It very much depends on the situation. In London today it would look differently than in Berlin during Hitler's rule or Moscow during Stalin's rule; and in Constantinople in the eighth century it would look differently than in Washington in the eighteenth century or in Bangalore today. In this text, I am interested in settings that are closer to London and Bangalore now—settings of rapid change, self-sufficiency of social subsystems, cultural pluralism, and diminished control—than they are either to Constantinople before its sack in 1453 or to Moscow during World War II.

Michel de Certeau's account of the uses people make of cultural goods produced for them may help us think about the nature of Christian public engagement in such settings. He writes, "Users make innumerable and infinitesimal transformations of and within the dominant cultural economy in order to adapt it to their own interests and their own rules."[27] He explains this creativity of users by examining an extreme case—the colonization of the indigenous American population that started on October 12, 1492, when Spanish ships sailed up to the shores of Latin America. We sometimes fail to see that in spite of its oppression and powerlessness, the indigenous population was not simply the passive recipient of an imposed culture. De Certeau writes:

> The Indians often used the laws, practices, and representations that were imposed on them by force or by fascination to ends other than those of their conquerors; they made something else out of them; they subverted them from within—not by rejecting them or by transforming them (though that occurred as well), but by many different ways of using them in the service of rules, customs, or convictions foreign to the colonization which they could not escape. They metaphorized the dominant order: they made it function in another register. They remained other within the system which they assimilated and which assimilated them externally. They diverted without leaving. Procedures of consumption maintained their difference in the very space that the occupier was organizing.[28]

The image of conquest and colonization is not fully adequate to describe the relation between cultures and Christian communities. For the culture is not simply an intruding power that one has to resist. It is a space in which one lives, the air one breathes. Leave the image of colonial imposition aside and attend to de Certeau's account of living within a dominant order. The main images are "metaphorizing" the culture, making it function in a different register, subverting it from within, using it to different ends, diverting from it without leaving, and so on. These are all ways of expressing the middle between abandoning and dominating the culture, of describing what it might mean to assert one's difference while remaining within it.

Now take de Certeau's basic idea of "leaving without departing" in its multiple variants and apply it to the relation of Christian communities to the wider culture. What are some paradigmatic options open to them? First, Christians can simply adopt some elements of the cultures in which they live. For example, there are no specifically Christian eating utensils. Whether one eats with fork and knife or with chopsticks is, as far as the Christian faith is concerned, utterly inconsequential (though the faith may nudge one to prefer well designed and well crafted utensils and those made using sustainable practices). But Christians will often use elements adopted from a culture in a different way, guided by the story of Jesus Christ. To stay with the example of eating practices, a meal can be an occasion for generosity and an expression of worship rather than an instance of individual or communal self-gratification. The character of the meal, then, changes. Indeed, even the character of the hunger itself changes. Karl Marx has famously written, "Hunger is hunger, but the hunger gratified by cooked meat eaten with a knife and fork is a different hunger from that which bolts down raw meat with the aid of hand, nail, and tooth."[29] Similarly, hunger gratified while sharing with strangers and worshiping God is a different hunger than the one gratified while concerned with one's own eating pleasure alone.[30]

Sometimes putting things to different uses might require alteration in things themselves. To be a good site of hospitality, a house might need a smaller master bedroom to accommodate a guest room and a larger living room—which brings me to the second possible way of living Christian difference within a given culture: the majority of the elements of a culture will be taken up but transformed from within.

What Christians do with language is a good example. Christians use the same language as the culture at large, but they infuse semantic fields of words with new content. "God" is the most

91

basic term in Christian vocabulary. Christians did not invent it; they inherited it from the Hebrew people of God, as they in turn adopted it from their cultural environment. Yet just as for Jews "God" came to mean "the God of Abraham and Sarah, the God of Moses and Miriam," so for Christians the semantic field of the term "God" partly changed to mean "the Father of Jesus Christ" and ultimately led to the understanding of God as the Holy One who is the Holy Three. Most Christian terms have undergone similar inner transformations.

The same is true of many Christian practices. Christians take part in culturally defined practices but shape them on the basis of their dominant values—rooted in the revelation of God in Jesus Christ. Take marriage as an example. Many of its elements are the same for Christians as they are for non-Christians of the same culture. Yet for Christians, the love between partners is an echo of the relationship between Christ and the church—both partners being willing to give themselves to the other and for the other, and in doing so loving both themselves and the other as themselves (see Eph. 5:21–33).

Third, there may be some elements of a culture that Christians will have to reject. The institution of slavery is a good example; it simply had to be discarded, even though slavery was initially only emptied of its inner content rather than directly abolished as a social institution. In Christ there is "no longer slave or free," but all are "children of God through faith" (Gal. 3:26–28). Philemon, the slave owner, should receive Onesimus, the runaway slave, as "a beloved brother," and not only "in the Lord" but also "in [the] flesh" (Philem. 16). When both master and slave mutually recognize each other as "beloved siblings"—and, to echo Georg W. F. Hegel, when they each recognize this mutual recognition[31]—slavery has been abolished even if its outer institutional shell remains as an oppressive reality.

From the three complementary ways of relating to culture, it follows that Christian identity in a culture is always a complex and flexible network of small and large refusals, divergences, subversions, and more or less radical and encompassing alternative proposals and enactments, surrounded by the acceptance of many cultural givens. There is no single way to relate to a given culture as a whole or even to its dominant thrust; there are only numerous ways of accepting, transforming, or replacing various aspects of a given culture from within. Christians never have their own *proper and exclusive* cultural territory—their own exclusive language, values, practices, or rationality. They speak the language they have learned from others, though they metaphorize its meaning. They inherit the value structure of the culture at large, yet they change more or less radically some of its elements and refuse to accept others. They take up the rules of a given culture, and yet they subvert them, change them partly, refuse to obey some of them, and introduce new ones.

To become a Christian means to divert without leaving. To live as a Christian means to keep inserting a difference into a given culture without ever stepping outside that culture to do so.

Two Noes and One Yes

Let me summarize in three terse propositions—two denials and one affirmation—my account of internal difference as a mode of Christian identity and engagement in contemporary societies.

No to Total Transformation

For Christian difference to be internal to a given culture means that Christians have no place from which to transform the *whole culture they inhabit*—no place from which to undertake that eminently modern project of restructuring the whole of social and intellectual life, no virgin soil on which to start building a new, radically different city.[32] No total transformations are possible; all transformations are reconstructions of the structures that must be inhabited as the reconstruction is going on. No total transformations are desirable. Consider the eschatological new Jerusalem Revelation describes as "coming down out of heaven from God" (21:2). It is not designed and built by Christians. And yet, it stands in continuity and not just discontinuity with the old order; it is said that the "people"—non-Christian people!—"will bring into it the glory and the honor of the nations" (21:26).[33]

What Christians end up building in the course of history does not resemble a modern city, like Brasilia, all designed and built from scratch. Instead, they are helping to build what resembles more of an ancient city with its "maze of little streets and squares, of old and new houses, and of houses with additions from various periods; and this surrounded by a multitude of new boroughs with straight regular streets and uniform houses."[34] This is how the philosopher Ludwig Wittgenstein describes human language. A similar kind of change over time happens when Christians insert themselves, along with many and varied non-Christians, into a given culture.

No to Accommodation

Accommodation to the broader culture should not be part of the Christian project, either. We are used to the rejection of accommodation from old-style fundamentalists. And in this regard they were right (though they often failed to live up to their own rhetoric and accommodated in rather predictable ways, only to different aspects of culture than their progressive competitors). The accommodation strategy has not worked, and, given the nature of contemporary societies, the likelihood that it will work in the future is negligible. What is worse, unless accompanied by robust affirmation of specific Christian identity—of Christian difference from a given culture!—accommodation carries in itself seeds of Christian self-dissolution.

If Christian identity matters, then difference must matter as well. In the most general sense, get rid of difference and what remains will be *nothing*—you yourself, along with everything else, will be drowned in the sea of undifferentiated "stuff." To erase difference is to undo the creation, that intricate pattern of separations and interdependencies that God established when the universe was formed out of *no*-thing. Literally, *every*-thing depends on difference.[35] Now apply this insight to the relation between the gospel and culture. Here too everything depends on difference. If you have difference, you have the gospel. If you don't, you will either have just plain old culture or the universal reign of God, but you won't have the gospel. The gospel is always also about difference; after all, it means the good news—something good, something *new*, and therefore something different!

But how should we "negotiate" Christian identity and difference in the midst of cultural change? First, Christian identity is established not primarily by denying and combating what is outside but by embracing and highlighting the center of what is inside—Jesus Christ as the Word who took on flesh and became the Lamb of God bearing the sin of the world. Difference matters not because uniqueness matters; when it comes to the Christian faith (unlike culture or personality), uniqueness is a non-value. Difference matters because and to the extent that identity matters. Put slightly differently, properly understood Christian identity is not reactive but positive; the center defines the difference, not fear of others, either of their uncomfortable proximity or their dangerous aggressiveness.

Second, relationship to what is outside should be governed by love. "For God so loved the world"—the world as God's good creation and the world as gone astray, even gone awry—and

95

sent Jesus Christ into the world to save it. Similarly, the followers of Jesus Christ are sent into the world as he was sent, to love friends and enemies, co-religionists and infidels, and to rejoice in everything that is true, good, and beautiful wherever they encounter it.

Third, boundaries must be permeable. Without boundaries, groups lose identity and abdicate any possibility of social impact. But the boundaries of Christian communities cannot be the impenetrable walls of tall fortresses. They must be open for traffic to go out (engagement for change) as well as in (appreciating the good that is outside and learning from it).

One way to make my point would be to say that accommodation happens whether you intend it or not; it is a given. Difference, as I understand it here, is an achievement, a conscious exercise in defining one's identity around the center of faith in dynamic give-and-take with surrounding cultures by practicing love of God and love of neighbor. The positive result of both de facto accommodation and conscious drawing of permeable boundaries is inculturation—an expression of the Christian faith in terms of the culture to which it comes and in which it takes root.

Yes to Engagement

The prophetic role of Christian communities—their engagement to mend the world, to foster human flourishing, and to serve the common good—is nothing but their identity projecting itself outward in word and deed. Two consequences follow.

First, the followers of Christ are *engaged* in the world *with their whole being*. Engagement is not a matter of either speaking or doing; not a matter of either offering a compelling intellectual vision or embodying a set of alternative practices; not a matter of either merely making manifest the richness and depth of interior life or merely working to change the institutions of society; not a matter of either only displaying alternative politics as gathered in Eucharistic celebrations or merely working for change as the dispersed people of God. It is all these things and more. The whole person in all aspects of her life is engaged in fostering human flourishing and serving the common good. Though it may be important to distinguish between private and public as well as individual and communal aspects of engagement, these dimensions are inextricably intertwined and form an inseparable unity.

Second, Christian engagement concerns *all dimensions of a culture*. It concerns, first, how the *self* is (implicitly or explicitly) understood and what it does in the interiority of its heart, in the privacy of its home, and in the open space of public life. Second, it concerns *social relations*—people's rights and obligations—in business, politics, entertainment, communication, and more. Finally, Christian engagement concerns the *vision of the good*—that which defines what we as individuals and societies should seek (and therefore also what we should try to avoid). Christian engagement touches all dimensions of a culture and yet doesn't aim to transform any of them totally. Instead, in all of them it also seeks and finds goods to be preserved and strengthened. It is total in scope but limited in extent—limited not just by resistance of individuals, social systems, and whole societies to change, but also limited by the finitude and fragility of humanity as well as by its inalienable goodness.

In the following two chapters, I explore two central modes of Christian public engagement: witness to non-Christians and participation in political life.

6

Sharing Wisdom

We live in an age of great conflicts and petty hopes.
Consider first our hopes. In the book *The Real American Dream*, Andrew Delbanco traces the history of the scope of American dreams—from the "holy God" of the Puritan founders, to the "great nation" of the nineteenth-century patriots, to the "satisfied self" of many today.[1] With some modifications, America may be in this regard indicative of trends in most societies that are highly integrated into the global market system. As I argued in chapter 4, the idea of flourishing as a human being has shriveled to meaning no more than leading an experientially satisfying life. The sources of satisfaction may vary: power, possessions, love, religion, sex, food, drugs—whatever. What matters most is not the *source* of satisfaction but the *experience* of it—*my* satisfaction. Our satisfied self is our best hope. Not only is this petty, but a dark shadow of disappointment stubbornly follows our obsession with personal satisfaction. We are meant to live for something larger than

our own satisfied selves. Petty hopes generate self-subverting, melancholy experiences.

Second, our world is caught in great conflicts (as well as in many small, even trivial ones). Many of these conflicts are fought along religious lines (which does not necessarily mean that they are primarily religious conflicts).[2] Christians and Muslims are clashing; so are Muslims and Jews, Hindus and Christians, Buddhists and Muslims, and so on, with the conflict between the Western world (shaped by Christianity) and the majority-Muslim world overshadowing them all. Although for the most part religions per se are not the causes of these conflicts, religions often legitimize and fuel them by enveloping mundane causes—sometimes our petty hopes—with an aura of the sacred.

Most religions see as one of their main goals the opening up of people to connect them with a broader community and, indeed, with the source and goal of all reality. Similarly, most religions claim to contain important, even indispensable resources for fostering a culture of peace. But these two functions of religions are sometimes at odds with one another. When distinct religions connect people with the divine, bring people together, and offer them a hope larger than mere self-fulfillment, communities with differing religious beliefs sometimes clash. When religions try to avoid legitimizing and fueling clashes between people, they often retreat into some private sphere and at times even reinforce people's self-absorption. This is a version of the tendency of religions in today's world to oscillate between coerciveness and idleness, which I note in chapter 1.

A central challenge for all religions in a pluralistic world is *to help people grow out of their petty hopes so as to live meaningful lives, and to help them resolve their grand conflicts and live in communion with others.* That's where the importance of learning to share religious wisdom well comes in. If we as religious people fail to share wisdom well, we will fail our many contemporaries who strive to live satisfied lives and yet remain deeply dissatisfied, and we will fail those who draw on their religious traditions to give meaning to their lives and yet remain mired in intractable and often deadly conflicts.

But how do we share religious wisdom well? I will address this question from a Christian perspective. Though there is no religiously generic way to share wisdom well (mainly because there is no generic religion), I hope that adherents of other religions will resonate with what I say, that they will find that it overlaps with how they believe the wisdom of their own traditions should be shared. But first let me say something about what, from that same perspective, wisdom is—and why people should share it.[3]

What Is Wisdom?

Christians have traditionally understood their faith not as a religious add-on to life but as itself constituting an integrated way of life.[4] Correspondingly, Christian wisdom in one sense is that faith itself—an overarching interpretation of reality, a set of convictions, attitudes, and practices that direct people in living their lives well. Here "living well" means living as God created human beings to live, rather than living against the grain of their own true reality and the reality of the world. Wisdom in this sense is an integrated *way of life* that enables the flourishing of persons, communities, and all creation (see chapter 4). Human beings are wise if they walk in that way.

Christians have also understood wisdom as something far more particular than a whole way of life—namely, as concrete *pieces of advice* about how to flourish. When we read in Proverbs, "A fool takes no pleasure in understanding but only in expressing personal opinion" (18:2), or when Jesus says, "Give, and it will be given to you" (Luke 6:38), or when the apostle Paul says, "Do not

101

worry about anything" (Phil. 4:6), or when we read in the Letter to the Ephesians, "Be kind to one another, tenderhearted, forgiving one another, as God in Christ has forgiven you" (4:32), we are presented with wise advice, with what one may call "nuggets" of wisdom. Properly understood, these nuggets are components of wisdom as a way of life. According to this sense of wisdom, human beings are wise if they follow wise advice.

There is yet a third and more basic way in which Christians understand wisdom—surprisingly, perhaps, wisdom is a *person*. In the book of Proverbs wisdom is personified. She is the very beginning of God's creation, and she calls out to humans to listen to her and to flourish by obeying her (Prov. 8). Christians have taken this "lady wisdom" to be the Word incarnate, Jesus Christ (John 1:1–14). The apostle Paul also writes that Jesus Christ "became for us wisdom from God" (1 Cor. 1:30). Here human beings are wise if they follow Christ and, even more fundamentally, if they allow that personified wisdom to dwell in them, conform them to itself, and act through them (Gal. 2:20).

In all three senses just described, wisdom is not a matter of personal taste or preference ("This strikes me as wise—for the time being!"), as "wisdom" often is for people in dynamic and ever-changing contemporary societies. Neither is wisdom a marker of a group identity, a kind of beneficent custom ("This is wisdom for us, though not necessarily for you"), as it might be for some more ethnic religions or cultures. For Christians, wisdom is a peculiar kind of *truth* that concerns all people—and concerns them in the deepest way. It concerns them as human beings, not as members of this or that group or as performers of certain tasks or pursuers of certain goals. To reject wisdom as a way of life, or Christ as the embodiment of wisdom, is not like leaving the dessert untouched after a good meal; rather, it is like refusing the very nourishment without which human beings cannot truly flourish.

This Christian claim is controversial, of course. Though it is not a negative statement about any religion or worldview, it is a claim that the Christian faith has the key to human beings succeeding not in this or that endeavor but in being human. But the aspect of it that a Muslim, for instance, might call into question is not the assertion that the wisdom of a particular religion is deemed indispensable, but that this claim applies to the Christian faith rather than to Islam. Controversial though it is, most Christians consider the claim necessary. Jewish monotheism introduced the idea of truth into the world of Western religions.[5] Christianity inherited that idea and radicalized it: the wisdom of faith is inextricably bound to the universal truth of faith; though supple and responsive to changing times and circumstances, that wisdom is valid for all people of all times.

For the sake of conciseness, when I explore in the following pages why and how to share wisdom, I will usually simply lump the three senses of wisdom together. The disadvantage of doing so is obvious: when it comes to why and how to share wisdom, the differences among these three senses of wisdom matter a great deal. The reasons for and manner of sharing wisdom when it is understood as nuggets of advice or as a way of life or as a divine Person only partly overlap. So I will point occasionally to differences in sharing wisdom in these three distinct senses, but I will have to leave it to the readers to fill in many blanks.

Why Share Wisdom?

What are the most important reasons for sharing wisdom?

First, Christians have an *obligation* to share wisdom. After his death and resurrection, Jesus Christ said to his disciples, "As the Father has sent me, so I send you" (John 20:21)—with a mission to announce the good news, and more broadly to share God's wisdom with the world. Christians share wisdom because Jesus Christ commanded them to do so.[6]

Second, the obligation to share wisdom is an expression of *love* for neighbors. Just as the Father's sending of Jesus was rooted in God's love for the world (John 3:16), so also is the Christian's mission rooted in love for fellow human beings—or at least it should be rooted in love. Christians share wisdom to help needy people find meaning in life or resolve conflicts, to offer reasons for feeding the hungry and clothing the naked, and in general because they desire to prevent others from languishing or even perishing as a result of living "out of sync" with the way in which God created them to live.[7]

Ultimately, however, Christians don't share wisdom merely out of obedience to a command, and not even simply out of love for neighbors. In reality they share it—or at least should share it—primarily because the wisdom dwelling in them *seeks to impart itself* through them to others. As the apostle Paul puts it, the "love of Christ urges [them] on" (2 Cor. 5:14).

These religious motivations to share wisdom *fit the character of the Christian faith*. As I noted earlier, along with some other major world religions, Christianity is a monotheistic faith of a prophetic type. Take first the significance of *monotheism* for sharing wisdom. When it comes to God's relation to the world, there is a strict correlation between the divine "One" and the mundane "whole." Since God is One, God is the God of the whole of reality. Though always concrete and attuned to specific situations, the wisdom of the one God is the wisdom for the whole of humanity, not just a segment of it. It should therefore be shared with all.

The thrust toward sharing generated by monotheism is reinforced by the prophetic character of the Christian faith. As I explain in chapter 1, religions of the prophetic type are structured by two basic movements: ascent to the realm of the divine (encounter with God, deep study of Scriptures, and the like) and return with a message for the world—a twofold movement illustrated well by the account in the Gospels according to which Jesus began his public ministry by fasting in the wilderness. In the ascent, religious persons acquire wisdom and are transformed; in the return, they share wisdom with fellow human beings in order to transform the world. The ascent doesn't happen simply so that the person would benefit from the encounter with God (as in mystical religions); it happens also for the purpose of the return, so that the world will be mended and brought into greater conformity with God's designs for it.

Christians have powerful reasons to share religious wisdom with others. And on the whole, throughout history they haven't shied away from doing so (though in some periods their cross-cultural missionary impulse has been subdued, as in the case of Protestants from their inception in 1517 to about 1794, when William Carey started the modern Protestant missionary movement).[8] There are situations, however, in which it may be unwise to share religious wisdom. In the Sermon on the Mount, Jesus Christ famously and harshly warns, "Do not give what is holy to dogs; and do not throw your pearls before swine, or they will trample them under foot and turn and maul you" (Matt. 7:6). These severe words are a reminder that relations between religions are sometimes very tense, even violent. In such circumstances—for example, of religious persecution, which has been historically and geographically widespread and in certain places continues unabated today[9]—sharing wisdom may elicit both angry incomprehension and further violence. Sometimes wisdom counsels not to be shared. At other times, notwithstanding the severity of opposition, courageous wisdom will cry out to be heard just so as to expose the foolishness of the opponents.

The Self as a Giver of Wisdom

When done well, sharing wisdom can be likened to the giving and receiving of gifts (see chapter 7). Before we go into the specifics of how to give and receive wisdom and how not to do so, note one important feature of sharing wisdom: it is more like playing a musical piece for a friend than treating her to a meal. When I serve a meal to a friend, what she eats I no longer have; in contrast, when I play music for her, she receives something that, in a sense, I continue to possess. When I share wisdom, I don't part with what I give; to the contrary, I may come to possess it in a deeper way.[10]

What does it mean to share wisdom well? How does one share it responsibly? I will explore these questions by examining how we should act both as givers and receivers of wisdom. From the very inception of the church, Christians witnessed publicly about their faith. The church was born on the day of Pentecost,[11] and on that occasion the disciples of the crucified and resurrected Jesus Christ spoke about him in many languages to people from many parts of the world. They actively shared the wisdom of their faith in all three of the senses outlined above—as nuggets, as a whole way of life, and as wisdom incarnate.

For Christians, giving *witness* is a key way of sharing wisdom. But what does it mean to witness well? First, a witness is *not a tyrant* who imposes. True, throughout history Christians have sometimes sought to impose their faith by the sword,[12] by the power of rhetorical manipulation, or with inducements of material gain. Yet imposition stands starkly at odds with the basic character of the Christian faith, which is at its heart about self-giving—God's self-giving and human self-giving—and not about self-imposing. Karl Barth, a great Protestant theologian of the past century, puts it correctly: in relation to non-Christians (and to fellow Christians!), followers of Christ are in the position of John the Baptist as depicted in the famous painting of

Matthias Grünewald—namely, at the foot of the cross with an outstretched hand simply pointing to the crucified Christ.[13] Far from imposing the wisdom of faith, they don't even offer it as something they themselves give—properly, they merely point to the wisdom. That wisdom offers itself; some will partake, and others refuse.[14]

Second, a witness is not a *merchant* who sells. Deeply enmeshed as we moderns are in economic exchanges, we live in cultures pervaded by the activity of buying and selling.[15] Often we treat religions and their wisdom as commodities to be bought and sold. Although there are good reasons to remunerate priests, pastors, and other religious leaders, neither they nor unpaid laypeople are sellers of wisdom—certainly they are no more sellers of wisdom than good teachers are sellers of knowledge or good doctors sellers of cures.[16] Wisdom is betrayed when it is sold and bought, and not just, as I will argue later, because it is fundamentally a gift. Sellers are tempted to seduce buyers into making a purchase by tailoring the merchandise to fit the desires of the buyer; the act of selling often distorts wisdom and leaves buyers with a festering suspicion that the seller has taken advantage of them. Buyers, on the other hand, pick and choose and purchase as much or as little as they see fit. When bought and sold, wisdom tends not to shape people's lives but at best merely to satisfy already existing desires—likely none of which wisdom itself has crafted, and to all of which wisdom is subservient. Treated as a commodity, wisdom deteriorates into a technique for helping people live the way they please, even when the way they please to live may be thoroughly unwise.[17]

In the Christian tradition at its best, wisdom is given freely. The prophet Isaiah writes, "Ho, everyone who thirsts come to the waters; and you that have no money, come, buy and eat! Come, buy wine and milk without money and without price" (Isa. 55:1). Jesus echoes these words when he says, "Come to me, all you that are weary and are carrying heavy burdens, and I will give you rest" (Matt. 11:28). Christian wisdom is fundamentally about what God gives free of charge and must therefore be imparted free of charge.[18] A good witness will resist the commodification of wisdom.

Third, as witnesses, Christians are not mere *teachers* who instruct. A teacher can learn something that remains very much external to her own life and then pass it on as useful information to others (say, in the way a math professor may teach trigonometry). Christians, in contrast, should witness as those who not only speak about Christ with their words but also imitate him in their behavior and entrust themselves to his care in their living and dying. When they witness, then, they are pointing to a way of life in which they themselves participate. Consequently, the more "indwelled" by wisdom they are, the better sharers of wisdom they will be.

Fourth, a witness is not a mere *midwife*. The great Greek teacher of wisdom Socrates saw himself in the role of a midwife. His task was to help birth the wisdom with which every person was already pregnant. He himself was incidental to the process of acquiring wisdom.[19] According to this view, if a person is sufficiently self-aware, she can find her own way to wisdom, for wisdom resides within her.

Not so with Christ, and not so with a witness to Christ. Christ does not help a person find the wisdom hidden in her own soul; Christ *is* the wisdom.[20] Consequently, a follower of Christ is a witness to Christ, whose purpose is to direct the attention of a person away from herself to Christ—to the life, death, and resurrection of the Word incarnate, who lived in a specific time and place. Socrates helps a person discover something inside herself, something she knew, had forgotten, and needed to be reminded of; in contrast, a witness to Christ tells a person about something that has occurred outside herself, something about which she must be informed.[21] So a witness points not only away from herself but also away from the person to whom she is giving witness; she points to Christ and the wisdom he was and continues to be.

The Other as Receiver

Good givers will respect the integrity of receivers. There are limits to what others may be willing or able to receive, and givers should honor these limits. Christians should share wisdom in the way that the first letter of Peter instructs them to give an account of their hope—"with gentleness and reverence" (1 Pet. 3:15–16).

It is relatively easy to honor others' limits when it comes to sharing nuggets of wisdom. The receivers can integrate these bits of wise advice into their own overarching interpretations of life without much disruption. Often, though, what is received takes on a different flavor from what is given. Chicken in Thai food tastes different from the way it tastes in a sandwich with mustard and mayonnaise. A nugget of wisdom in one "dish" of religion will taste different when served with different ingredients. More prosaically put, receivers will often gratefully receive what is offered but tweak it to fit into their overarching interpretation of life.

Granting the right of others to receive what they want and do with it as they see fit is part of the respect that givers afford to recipients. There is some reason for concern, however, about sharing one's nuggets of wisdom in the fast-paced, media-saturated, salad-bar culture in which many of us live. First, givers themselves often dilute their wisdom to make it palatable to as many receivers as possible. Second, receivers often do not insert newly acquired nuggets of wisdom into an overarching interpretation of life. The nuggets remain free-floating bits of advice that are used when convenient and discarded when not. This selective employment of wisdom out of context may then contribute to making an unwise way of life more viable—certainly not the goal of sharing wisdom!

Sharing wisdom as a way of life becomes even more complicated. The most significant limits to what others are able to receive are set by their fear of losing their identity. For if they take too much from the "outside," their reception of wisdom may feel like an unwelcome undoing of their very selves. To receive Christ as wisdom or to receive faith as a way of life may seem profoundly alienating to the would-be taker. But it goes without saying in a chapter written by a Christian on sharing wisdom that embracing a Christian way of life *can be*, and *mostly is*, experienced as a return to our own proper selves.

The Christian tradition has always accepted the real possibility that others may see the highest wisdom to which it points as utter foolishness. A way of life in which self-giving is praised and the exercise of power over others is suspected appears to some as folly, not wisdom.[22] So also does the idea that Jesus Christ saves through his death on the cross.[23] Wisdom may not appear wise at first. For people to recognize it *as* wisdom, they must have some affinity with it—they must have eyes to see and ears to hear, as the prophet Ezekiel puts it (Ezek. 12:1–2).[24] That's why some important strands of the Christian tradition suggest that people can receive wisdom only when God's Spirit creates in them the right conditions for its reception.[25]

Notice that in two crucial regards—at the point of giving and at the point of receiving—it is not Christians themselves who do the most important work in sharing wisdom. Ultimately they cannot give it, for Christ must give wisdom. And ultimately they cannot make others receive wisdom; God's Spirit must open people's eyes to see it. When Christians are at their best in sharing wisdom, they are channels through which God imparts wisdom. The book of Acts expresses this basic idea clearly when reporting the first conversions to the way of Christ: it wasn't the apostles who converted people through their preaching—it was *God* who added people to the church (Acts 2:47).

The Self as Receiver

As we share the wisdom of our religious tradition, we should keep in mind that the person to whom we offer wisdom is also a giver, not just a passive receiver. As givers, we respect receivers by seeing ourselves as potential receivers too. Yet many religious people find it difficult to think of themselves as receiving anything of substance from people of other faiths. After all, they are already embracing what they likely believe is a—even *the*—true and salutary way of life. That perspective is certainly true of many Christians. Doesn't John's Gospel say that Christ is "the way, and the truth, and the life" (14:6)? Doesn't the Letter to the Colossians state that in Christ are "hidden all the treasures of wisdom and knowledge" (2:3)? How, then, can Christians receive any significant wisdom from others?

This question is suggesting that receiving wisdom from others might not be possible, when that has in fact indisputably already taken place! It isn't at all difficult to demonstrate that Christians have received wisdom from others in the past and that they continue to do so. Two examples from the distant past will suffice. The first is Christianity's appropriation of the spiritual treasures of Judaism. With some minor modifications, for instance, the Christian Old Testament is the Hebrew Bible, made up of texts that by themselves comprised the sacred Scriptures of the early Christians. Second, Christianity's early encounter with Greek language and culture meant its inevitable (though for the most part unintentional) receiving of Greek wisdom.[26] A rich vocabulary of faith comes to the theology and everyday liturgical life of Christians from the Greek philosophical tradition (even if major philosophical terms have been partly transformed when appropriated).[27] Indeed, more broadly than in Christianity's encounter with ancient Greek culture, the Christian faith has received wisdom every time the gospel has been translated into another language and taken root in a different cultural environment.[28]

So how can Christians, who believe that all wisdom resides in and emanates from Jesus Christ, receive the wisdom of others? The answer, though not obvious to all, is simple even if it is not easy to see all its implications. Jesus Christ is the incarnate Word—wisdom!—through whom "all things came into being" and who is "the light of all people," as one of the most influential texts of the New Testament, the prologue to the Gospel of John, puts it (John 1:3–4). Echoing the text of John's Gospel, early church father Justin Martyr describes the wisdom of Greek philosophers as "parts of the Word" and "seeds of truth."[29] All light, wherever encountered, is the light of the Word and therefore Christ's light; all wisdom, whoever speaks it, is Christ's wisdom. It cannot be otherwise if *all things* come into being and exist through the Word who became incarnate in Christ. Granted, that's a big "if," one that non-Christians will be unwilling to accept. But at issue here are the stances of Christians, not their plausibility to non-Christians. Accept the condition ("all things came into being" through Christ), and the consequence ("all wisdom is Christ's wisdom") follows ineluctably.

But Christians already have Christ, one could object. Why accept anything from others, even if one grants that they possess "seeds" of wisdom? First, there is a depth and breadth to Christ, the wisdom, that remain always unplumbed by his followers. Put somewhat more abstractly, the object of faith—God, who dwells in inapproachable light—is never fully present in the consciousness and practice of the faithful, even the most enlightened ones, not just because they are finite creatures and God is the infinite Creator, but because they are all driven by their own needs and proclivities and shaped by the particular situations in which they live. Second, along with others, Christians live in a stream of time that throws at human beings ever-new challenges. Often they find themselves disoriented and uncertain as to how to bring the wisdom of Christ to bear upon new situations, how to be wise in the ever-changing here and now. They may think of themselves as wise while they are in fact foolish. That's why what Paul Tillich called "reverse prophetism"[30] is sometimes indispensable: Christians can (and often should) receive from the outside a prophetic challenge to alter their convictions and practices so as to live in the here and now more consistently with the wisdom they embrace.[31]

As the relationship between "the Word" and "parts of the Word" suggests, any wisdom that Christians receive from others must resonate with the scriptural narratives about Christ. Compatibility between these multifaceted narratives and the inexhaustible treasure of meanings is for Christians the criterion that determines what is wisdom and what is not, what may come in and what must stay out. Of course, it is possible to give up on these narratives—indeed, one may come to believe that it would be foolish *not* to give up on them. But a person who comes to this conclusion has abandoned the Christian faith either in favor of another way of life (say, Jainism or the philosophy of Nietzsche) or in favor of relating to all ways of life in the manner in which she approaches a salad bar—picking and choosing what suits her and disregarding the rest.

Sharing Wisdom: Love and Forgiveness

One way to describe what I have suggested in the main body of this chapter is to say that the sharing of wisdom should be an enactment of neighborly love.

When we share wisdom, we give and receive, and giving and receiving should be an exercise in love. Jesus Christ, the wisdom, is the embodiment of God's love for humanity, and he summed up both "the law and the prophets" and the "love command" when he issued the Golden Rule: "In everything do to others as you would have them do to you" (Matt. 7:12). "Everything" encompasses the sharing of wisdom. For neighborly love to define how wisdom should be shared means that the act of sharing wisdom harmonizes with the content of what is shared.[32]

As mentioned earlier, however, over the centuries Christians have sometimes shared wisdom in ways diametrically opposed to the requirements of the very wisdom they have inherited—manipulatively, forcibly, even murderously.[33] Similarly, Christians themselves have suffered greatly from the imposition of others' wisdom on them. Claims that more Christians were persecuted and killed on account of their faith in the past one hundred years than in the entire prior history of the church may be exaggerated,[34] but persecutions of Christians under Lenin and Stalin in the Soviet Union and Mao in China were brutal and massive by all accounts.[35]

When human beings are wronged, as in such relations between Christians and non-Christians, forgiveness and repentance are called for. That's what Christian wisdom teaches. The injunction to forgive may seem like just one "nugget" of Christian wisdom. It is that but also much more. It is the defining stance of Jesus Christ, wisdom personified, and a central pillar of the Christian way of life.[36]

Let me briefly note some key elements of forgiveness and relate them to the wronging that happens when Christians and adherents of other religions share wisdom poorly. Forgiveness itself is like a gift. And just as a gift must be received in order to be truly given, so also must forgiveness. We receive forgiveness by repenting—by naming our objectionable deeds as wrongs, by grieving over the injury inflicted, and by determining to mend our ways. It is crucial for Christians to examine honestly the way they have shared their wisdom in the past, see themselves in the proper light—purify their memory, as the late Pope John Paul II put it[37]—and, where appropriate, admit to wrongs and correct their ways. Of course, non-Christians would do well to do the same. Still, in cases of mutual wronging, Christian wisdom says that one's repentance does not depend on that of the other party. If we have wronged each other, I need to repent regardless of whether you repent.

More radically, Christian wisdom teaches that forgiveness itself, and not just repentance, doesn't even depend on the repentance of the wrongdoer—a notion that presses the limits of what other traditions might be willing or able to receive from the Christian tradition. Human beings were reconciled to God in Christ apart from their repentance. "Christ died for the ungodly"—*all* ungodly—writes the apostle Paul (Rom. 5:6). So also, the followers of Christ should forgive apart from wrongdoers' repentance. We give the gift of forgiveness properly not as a reward for repentance but in the hope that the gift itself will help the wrongdoer to receive it by repenting. Forgiving and sharing wisdom are similar in this one important regard: they are forms of gift giving. By giving a gift, one always acts first—and then waits expectantly to see whether or not the other will freely receive it.

Why forgiveness first, and then repentance? Because the goal of forgiveness is not simply to lighten the forgiver's psychological burden, not even simply to diffuse conflict, but to return the offender to the good and, ultimately, to restore communion between the wrongdoer and the wronged. Those who follow Christ, writes Martin Luther,

> grieve more over the sin of their offenders than over the loss or offense to themselves. And they do this that they may recall

those offenders from their sin rather than avenge the wrongs they themselves have suffered. Therefore they put off the form of their own righteousness and put on the form of those others, praying for their persecutors, blessing those who curse, doing good to the evil-doers, preparing to pay the penalty and make satisfaction for their very enemies that they may be saved. This is the gospel and the example of Christ.[38]

When Christians are wronged in the process of sharing wisdom—or more broadly, in any encounters with others—they ought to forgive. To forgive is to do two things at once: first, it is to name a suffered wrong *as* wrong. To forgive isn't to deny or even overlook the wrongdoing but rather to condemn it. No forgiveness without condemnation. But if condemnation is a necessary presupposition of forgiveness, the heart of forgiveness is something else. So to forgive is, second, not to let the wrongdoing count against the wrongdoer. He deserves punishment, but he gets the opposite. He gets grace.

Since forgiveness lies at the heart of Christian wisdom, as the above quotation from Martin Luther aptly expresses, for Christians to refuse to forgive is not just to fail to repair a short circuit in the sharing of wisdom—it is to contradict wisdom itself. To forgive *is* to share wisdom—perhaps it is even among the most efficacious ways of doing so.

Sharing Wisdom: Grand Conflicts, Petty Hopes

In conclusion, let me return to grand conflicts and petty hopes. How should we share wisdom so as not to reinforce religious conflicts but instead to help sustain and promote peace? We need to resist the temptation to "help" wisdom gain a footing in people's lives by manipulating or forcing others to embrace wisdom. Similarly, we need to resist the lure of pridefully perceiving ourselves as only givers of wisdom rather than also as

116

its receivers—and receivers from both expected and unexpected sources. If we give in to these tendencies, we will add to conflicts rather than preparing the soil in which faith can help resolve them. From a Christian perspective, all our efforts at sharing wisdom should focus on allowing wisdom to shape our own lives—including making us willing to both repent and forgive—and show itself in all its attractiveness, reasonableness, and usefulness. We need to trust that it will make itself embraceable by others if it is going to be embraced at all. In that way, as sharers of wisdom we honor both the power of wisdom and the integrity of its potential recipients.

How should we share wisdom so as not to feed petty hopes but instead to help persons connect meaningfully with communities—small and large—and with the source and goal of the universe? We need to resist the temptation to "package" religious wisdom in attractive and digestible "nuggets" that a person can take up and insert into a doomed project of striving to live a merely experientially satisfying life, a tendency prevalent especially in cultures shaped significantly by globalization processes. If we were to do so, wisdom would serve folly. From a Christian perspective, sharing religious wisdom makes sense only if that wisdom is allowed to counter the multiple manifestations of self-absorption by givers and receivers alike and to connect them with what ultimately matters—God, whom we should love with all our being, and neighbors, whom we should love as ourselves.

7

Public Engagement

Flourishing Religions

The world has always been a very religious place, and, by all appearances, it will continue to be in the foreseeable future. But as I note above, that's not what some of the great figures of European modernity expected. They thought that religion would, in one way or another, "wither away," to use a phrase that the Marxist tradition most commonly employed to describe the expected disappearance of the state in communist society.[1] Religion is irrational, the thinking went. It will take flight in the face of reason, just as the night's darkness takes flight before the dawn of a new day.[2] Religion is epiphenomenal. Ultimately, it causes nothing and explains nothing; in fact, other things, such as poverty, weakness, and oppression, cause and explain religion.[3] Once people, armed with knowledge and technological prowess, take their destinies into their own hands, religion will disappear. This is, very roughly, the basic content of the so-called secularization thesis—at least the part of it that concerns the continuation of religious beliefs and practices.

The secularization thesis has proven wrong, however. Or rather, it has proven only partially right, and that only in a very circumscribed set of societies—those of Western Europe and at a particular time in history. Even in these societies, religion has not quite withered away, but it wields significantly less influence now than it did a century ago. But contrary to all expectations, the rest of the world does not seem to be following a Western European pattern.[4] As Charles Taylor has rightly noted, it is now obvious that we can no longer speak of a single modernity that started in Europe and is spreading to the rest of the world, with secularization in its trail. There are many non-Western ways to modernize. Following Shmuel Eisenstadt,[5] Taylor speaks of "multiple modernities."[6] In most of these, economic progress, technological advances, and the increase and spread of knowledge sit quite comfortably alongside a thriving religion.

Worldwide, the fastest-growing overarching perspective on life is not secular humanism. If half a century ago secular humanism seemed to be the wave of the future, it's partly because in many places it was imposed from above by authoritarian and totalitarian governments—in the Soviet Union and Eastern European countries, in China, and in some Southeast Asian countries. There, secular humanism functioned like a parody of its originally imagined self: in the name of freedom—freedom from ignorance and oppression—secular humanism was imposed as an unquestioned ideology to legitimize oppression on a scale larger than history has ever seen.

In fact, the fastest-growing worldviews today are religious[7]—Islam and Christianity. And for the most part, they are propagated not by being imposed from above but by a groundswell of enthusiasm to pass the faith on and a thirst to receive it. Behind the spread of Christianity—behind the fact that Christianity is now predominantly a non-Western religion with over two billion adherents and growing mainly through conversion—is neither the power of states, nor the power of economic centers, nor the power of media or knowledge elites. Experts on world Christianity seem unanimous that the masses of believers are themselves the chief agents of its spread.[8]

As the mention of Christianity and Islam signals, the world is not just a religious place. It is a religiously *diverse* place. In addition to these two largest and fastest-growing religions, there are many relatively smaller religions that continue to thrive, Buddhism being the prime example. Moreover, within Christianity and Islam, there are many varied, sometimes even widely discordant movements. Finally, secular humanism itself in its diverse forms is also part of the world's religious diversity in that it shares with other religions one important feature: it comprises an overarching perspective on life (particularly some of its influential forms, such as Marxism).

Religious Diversity

An important social shift is underfoot in Western societies in regard to religion. Until recently, Western societies were relatively religiously homogenous. For centuries, they were predominantly Christian. Of course, there was always a small but significant presence of Jews, with whom relations ranged from overt and sometimes deadly hostility (as in Nazi Germany) to tolerance and friendliness (as in the post–World War II United States). And for centuries, Western Christianity itself was divided, or, in sociological speak, internally differentiated. Catholics, Protestants, Lutherans, Reformed, Anabaptists, Episcopalians, Methodists, Baptists, Pentecostals, and Seventh-Day Adventists coexisted, often in competition for membership and social influence. And

121

yet with the exception of Jews, a shared religious culture united them.

Slowly but steadily, the swath of that common religious culture is diminishing. Take the United States as an example: it has a robust Christian presence uncharacteristic of the rest of the Western world. Although Christianity is still by far the predominant religion here, others have a significant presence too. In addition to about 5.2 million Jews and about 31.6 million nonreligious people, there are about 2.5 million Muslims, perhaps 2.1 million Buddhists, and 1.2 million Hindus, to name just the most populous faiths.[9] In Europe too religions other than Christianity are growing, especially Islam. In the Western world, in the foreseeable future non-Christian religions will continue to increase in both absolute and relative terms.

And these numbers aren't significant only as indicators of the vitality of religions. They're also indicators of their potential political influence. Muslims, for instance, are numerous enough to be a significant political force, especially in Europe.[10] Moreover, they and other religious groups have both the social power and will to make their voices heard and to have their interests taken seriously. In the West, religiously pluralistic social spaces are likely to give rise to increasingly religiously pluralistic political bases and actors.

The workplace is a good site to observe the growing significance of religious plurality. In terms of religious diversity, it is a nearly exact though somewhat smaller replica of the wider culture. But it's not just that diverse religions are represented. Believers are also increasingly willing to bring their religious concerns into the office space or onto the factory floor. It used to be that workers hung their religion on a coatrack alongside their coats. At home, their religion mattered; at work, it was idle. This is no longer the case. For many people, religion has something to say about all aspects of life, work included.

Indeed, some of them are excellent workers precisely because they are devoutly religious.[11] But if religion is allowed into an office or factory, many religions will come—possibly as many as are represented in the workforce. This leads to interesting questions, such as how to configure a work space that is equally friendly to all religions. Religious diversity in the workplace is emerging as a significant issue analogous to racial or gender diversity.

The religious diversity of Western countries increasingly mirrors religious diversity in the world as a whole. At the level of individual nations, religious diversity is, of course, not a Western phenomenon. In a sense, it's a latecomer to the West. Some non-Western countries, such as India, have lived for centuries with religious pluralism.[12] Others are likely to become increasingly pluralistic, with various religions—foremost Christianity and Islam—competing for members and vying for social power and political influence. Globally and nationally, religious diversity will continue to be an important issue in the years to come. A modernist longing for a secular world is bound to be disappointed, just as the nostalgia for a "Christian Europe"[13] or a "Christian America"[14] is bound to remain just that: an unfulfilled nostalgia.

Religion in Liberal Democracy

Liberal democracy, a political project shared by both "conservatives" and "progressives," emerged in the West as an attempt to accommodate diverse religious perspectives on life within a single polity. It is democracy because governance is ultimately vested in adult citizens, each of whom has an equal voice. It is liberal because its two key ideas, in addition to equal protection before the law, are (1) freedom for each person to live in accordance with his or her own interpretation of life (or lack

123

of it), and (2) the state's neutrality with respect to all such perspectives on life.

In an essay entitled "The Role of Religion in Decision and Discussion of Political Issues," Nicholas Wolterstorff notes one pervasive, though not defining, feature of liberal democracies. In debates and decisions concerning political issues, citizens are not to base their positions on religious convictions derived from explicit divine revelation (from so-called positive revelation).[15] Instead,

> when it comes to such activities, they are to allow their religious convictions to idle. They are to base their political decisions and their political debate in the public space on the principles yielded by some source *independent of* any and all of the religious perspectives to be found in society.[16]

Wolterstorff also notes that those who advocate such idling of religious convictions in public matters often interpret the state's neutrality with respect to all religions as the *separation* of church and state—the famous "wall of separation."[17]

But for many religious people, it is part and parcel of their religious commitment to base their convictions about public matters on religious reasons—on Torah, on the teachings of the Old and New Testaments, or on the Qur'an, for instance. How can they be free to live the way they see fit when they aren't allowed to bring religious reasons into public debates and decisions? For these people, liberalism conceived in this way is illiberal. It hinders them from living out their lives as the faith they embrace urges them to.[18]

When religion leaves the public square—or is driven from it—the public square doesn't remain empty. Instead, it becomes filled with a diffuse phenomenon called secularism. Today in the West (unlike in the Soviet Union of the past century), secularism is not, strictly speaking, an ideology but rather a set of related values and truth-claims partly inherited selectively from the tradition, partly generated by the marketplace, and partly drawn from the hard sciences. The marketplace enthrones personal preference as the paramount value, and the hard sciences offer explanations using inner-worldly causalities as the only truth. With religions absent from the public square, secularism of this sort becomes the overarching perspective. My point here is not that secularism isn't admissible and respectable as such. It's rather that, by barring religious reason from public decision making and enforcing separation of church and state, secularism ends up as the *favored* overarching perspective—which is clearly unfair toward religious folks.

As an alternative, Wolterstorff suggests a form of liberal democracy he describes as "consocial." It has two main features. First, "it repudiates the quest for an independent source and it places no moral restraint on the use of religious reason. And second, it interprets the neutrality requirement, that the state be neutral with respect to the religious and other comprehensive perspectives present in society, as requiring *impartiality* rather than *separation*."[19] "What unites these two themes," Wolterstorff continues, "is that, at both points, the person embracing the consocial position wishes to grant citizens, no matter what their religion or irreligion, as much liberty as possible to live out their lives as they see fit."[20]

What also unites these two themes is advocacy of "a politics of multiple communities."[21] The liberal who bars religious reasons from public debate and advocates separation of church and state is clinging to "the politics of a community with shared perspective."[22] But Western nations are no longer such communities, if they ever truly were. They are communities made up of adherents of multiple religions and perspectives on life. In a polity that calls itself liberal, each of these should have a right to speak in the public square in a voice of its own.

Will religious communities support a polity in which they can speak in their own religious voices in the public arena and in which the state relates to all communities impartially? Elsewhere I have developed the argument that the monotheism of the Abrahamic faiths in fact favors the pluralistic political arrangements that liberal democracy, as understood by Wolterstorff, represents. Basically, the bare-bones sketch of the argument goes like this:

1. Because there is one God, all people are related to that one God on equal terms.
2. The central command of that one God is to love neighbors—to treat others as we would like them to treat us, as expressed in the Golden Rule.
3. We cannot claim any rights for ourselves and our group that we are not willing to give to others.
4. Whether as a stance of the heart or as outward practice, religion cannot be coerced.[23]

If you accept these four propositions, you have good reasons to support pluralism as a political project.

Will religious communities actually be willing to embrace such a political project? It depends on many factors. They are most likely to do so as minorities, who have a stake in their voice being heard. If one of them constitutes a majority, it may resist pluralism as a political project if its primary interest is maintenance of its privileged status. But if it is willing to follow the clear implications of its core theological and moral convictions, it will embrace pluralism as a political project. And certainly, unless religious communities are highly secularized, most of them will be likely to support such a polity more readily than one that is implicitly secular and therefore favors a perspective on life other than theirs. To be sure, some religions will strive to be favored by the state. But when they do, they are in principle no different than secularism is now or than secularism would continue to be under the "consocial" proposal. There are legal checks against favoring one perspective on life over others, and all players will have to face the moral demands of fairness and impartiality.

Liberal democracy, the kind that sought to take the convictions of particular religions out of public life, emerged in the wake of the European religious wars of the seventeenth century. People clashed partly because they had differing perspectives on life. To remove the cause of conflict, liberal democracy said the protagonists' religious perspectives should no longer be part of their public encounters. But if we are to live with a politics of multiple communities that bring their religious perspectives to the common table, as Wolterstorff suggests, won't violent clashes return? Under these conditions, is there a way of avoiding the return of religious conflict, even religious wars?

No Common Core

One way to avoid clashes triggered by particular religious perspectives would be to suggest that all religions are fundamentally the same. On the surface, the differences among them are obvious—from dress codes to arcane points of doctrine. But in this view, all such differences are an external husk containing the same kernel. All of them are media, conditioned by the particularities of indigenous cultures that communicate the same basic content. "Lamps are different, but the light is the same," said an old Muslim sage,[24] giving poetic expression to this account of the relations among religions. Its contemporary proponents have christened it "pluralist."[25]

The pluralist account of relations among religions fits rather nicely into the role assigned to religion by liberal democracy as currently understood. Just as liberal democracy relegates

127

particular religious perspectives to the private sphere, so the pluralist account of relations among religions relegates them to being accidental features of a given culture. In both cases, particularity is rendered idle—in the case of liberal democracy, by leaving it behind in favor of a universally accessible "independent source," and in the case of the pluralist account of religions, by seeing through religious particularities to the "common light" contained in all of them. More precisely, in both cases religious particularities can be acceptable to the degree that they are an instantiation of something more encompassing—public reason, in liberal democracy, and the heart of generic religious faith, in the pluralist account.

But the pluralist account of relations among religions is incoherent.[26] I don't mean here that it never ends up making good on its promise of including everyone on equal terms, although this is true too. Some religious group always ends up excluded, mainly because the teachings and practices of concrete religions are not only different but sometimes outright contradictory and stubbornly refuse to let themselves be interpreted as instances of an underlying sameness. We can expand the circle of the included, but we cannot avoid excluding—unless we declare every religion to be acceptable in advance. From my perspective, pluralists *rightly* exclude some; otherwise we would end up having to indiscriminately affirm anything and everything. Pluralists shouldn't pretend, however, to have overcome religious exclusivism.

The main trouble with the pluralist account of the relations among religions is that it tries to reduce religious diversity—that is, diversity that is acceptable on its own terms—to an underlying sameness. It offers a framework more overarching than any other in which each religion, and all of them together, are situated and of which they are made culturally specific instantiations. But such frameworks always squeeze particular religions into a preassigned mold, which is all the more troubling because for most religious folks, *their religion is itself the most encompassing framework for life and thought*. Attempts to reduce what's important in different religions to the same common core are bound to be experienced as disrespecting each religion in its particularity.

Religions simply don't have a common core—a crucial claim that I must leave undefended here. Each is composed of a set of loosely related rituals, practices, and metaphysical, historical, and moral claims to truth. Among different religions, these rituals, practices, and claims partly overlap (for instance, Muslims and Christians believe in one God) and partly differ (Muslims engage in ritual washings before prayers, for instance, and Christians don't), and are also partly mutually contradictory (most Muslims object to the Christian claim that Jesus died on the cross).

Moreover, there is no reason to think that the overlaps, differences, and disagreements in the future will be the same as they were in the past. Religions are dynamic, not static. They develop not only by interfacing with other domains of life, such as economic conditions or technological advances, but they also develop in mutual interaction with one another (and they do so especially in a globalized world).[27] To continue with the example of Christianity and Islam, we can trace the history of their encounters as a history of their shifting convergences and divergences. For centuries, for instance, it was uncontested that Muslims and Christians believe in the same God; at the beginning of the twenty-first century, the issue has become a highly contentious one.[28] Moreover, there has always been and still is a give-and-take between them, sometimes triggered by hostilities and sometimes facilitated by the friendliness of their adherents.

The dynamic character of each religion and the overlaps between them give some reason to hope that the perspectives of various people of faith need not always clash, or need not always clash fruitlessly, and that when the perspectives do clash, the people who hold them need not be mired in endless violence. But that's a hope; that's a possibility. What would it take to make it a reality? What would it take for religions not only to preserve their differences but to bring the wisdom of their own traditions to bear on public decisions and debates? What would it look like to do this and yet live in peace within a single democratic framework in which the law of the land treated members of all religions equally and the state related to all religious communities impartially?

Speaking in One's Own Voice

I have suggested that each person should speak in the public arena in his or her own religious voice. But what does it mean to speak in one's own voice? The answer has two components, one that is common to all religions and one that is specific to each.

If we think that all religions are basically the same, then what truly matters in each will be the same in all. To speak authentically as a religious person would mean to express in one's own idiom that which is common to all religious people. Disagreements that remain between people would be a function of something other than religion. But I've already noted that such an account of the relations among religions is implausible. Religions are irreducibly distinct.

An alternative view about what it means to speak in one's own religious voice takes an opposite tack and seizes on religious differences. What's important in each tradition is the way it differs from others. According to this view, to speak in a Christian voice would be to highlight what is specific to Christianity and leave out what is shared with other religions as comparatively unimportant. Whenever people of different religions entered public debate, their views, if they were religiously informed, would clash. But I've already suggested that religions don't just differ among themselves. They also agree, and they agree on some important issues.

Both approaches are wrongheaded because *they abstract from the concrete character of the religions themselves*, the one by zeroing in on what is claimed to be the same in all religions and the other by zeroing in on what is different. They miss precisely what is most important about a religion: *the particular configuration of its elements*, which may overlap with, differ from, or contradict some elements of other religions.[29] If one affirmed one's religion in this kind of particularity, what would it mean to speak in one's own voice?

To speak in a Muslim voice, for instance, would be neither to give a variation on a theme common to all religions nor to make exclusively Muslim claims in distinction from all other religions; it would give voice to Muslim faith in its concreteness, whether what it said overlapped with, differed from, or contradicted what people speaking in a Jewish or Christian or any other voice were saying (which is an echo in interfaith relations of the more general stance of religious communities toward culture that I suggest in chapter 5). Since truth matters, and since a false pluralism of approving pats on the back is cheap and short-lived, adherents of various religions will rejoice in overlaps and engage each other on differences and incompatibilities.

But if differences and incompatibilities remain in spite of significant agreements, then what will prevent clashes? Won't religious people, if they bring their differing and diverging perspectives into a public arena, plunge the political community into violence? For some, even to raise this question is to suggest that religious voices should be muted in the public domain and that some form of secularism should be embraced. But secularism won't help. It is just another perspective on life that isn't above the clashes but participates in them as one player, as the clashes between secularists and Muslims in Europe clearly show.[30] Moreover, when it comes to violence, the track record of secularism is no better than that of religions. Most violence perpetrated in the twentieth century—the most violent century in humanity's history—was done in the name of secular causes.

The only way to attend to the problem of violent clashes among differing perspectives on life—whether religious or secular—is to concentrate on the internal resources of each for fostering a culture of peace.[31] For each, these resources would be different, though again they may significantly overlap.

In regard to the Christian faith—the faith I embrace and study and the faith that is a good contender for having a legacy as violent as any other—developing its resources for fostering a culture of peace would mean at least two things. The first concerns the *center* of faith. From the very start, at the center of Christian faith was some version of the claim that God loved the sinful world and that Christ died for the ungodly (John 3:16; Rom. 5:6), and that Christ's followers must love their enemies no less than they love themselves. Love doesn't mean agreement and approval; it means benevolence and beneficence, possible disagreement and disapproval notwithstanding. A combination of moral clarity that does not shy away from calling evil by its proper name and of deep compassion toward evildoers that is willing to sacrifice one's own life on their behalf was one of the extraordinary features of early Christianity.[32] It should also be the central characteristic of contemporary Christianity.

The second consideration about speaking in a Christian voice follows from the first, and it concerns the nature of *identity*.[33] Every discrete identity is marked by boundaries. Some things are in, others are out; if all things were in or all things out, nothing particular would exist, which is to say that nothing

132

finite would exist at all—no boundaries, no identity, and no finite existence. The same holds true with regard to religions. And yet, that is not all that needs to be said about boundaries. Though necessary, boundaries should not be impermeable. In encounters with others, boundaries are always crossed, in fact, even if only minimally. People and communities with dynamic identities will have firm but permeable boundaries. With such boundaries, encounters with others don't serve only to assert our position and claim our territory; they are also occasions to learn and to teach, to be enriched and to enrich, to come to new agreements and maybe reinforce the old ones, and to dream up new possibilities and explore new paths. This kind of permeability of religious individuals and communities when they engage one another presupposes a basically positive attitude toward the other—an attitude in sync with the command to love the neighbor and, perhaps especially, to love the enemy.

To speak in one's own religious voice is to speak out of the center of one's faith. To speak in a Christian voice is to speak out of these two fundamental convictions: that God loves all people, including the transgressors, and that religious identity is circumscribed by permeable boundaries. Everything else that is said about every topic should be said informed by these two convictions. When that happens, the voice that speaks will be properly Christian but might contain nonetheless the echoes of many other voices, and many other voices will resonate with it. Of course, sometimes the voice will find no resonances, only contestation. That's the stuff good arguments are made of, in personal encounters as well as in the public sphere.

Exchanging Gifts

In 1779, Gotthold Ephraim Lessing published a small book entitled *Nathan the Wise*. The book was an instant success. It is a play set in twelfth-century Jerusalem about the relationships among the three Abrahamic faiths: Judaism, Christianity, and Islam. But its main theme is gift giving. The Muslim ruler of Jerusalem, Sultan Saladin, pardons a young Knight Templar who then rescues Resha, a daughter of a wealthy Jew by the name of Nathan who himself had adopted Resha when she was an orphaned Christian baby. All this giving among representatives of different religions—and much more—has one purpose: to underscore that it takes *generosity* for Jews, Christians, and Muslims to live in peace with one another.

In fact, Lessing makes two points about relations among the Abrahamic faiths, one negative and one positive. The negative one is that we can safely put aside debates about the truth-claims of religions. Adherents of each religion believe that their religion is true. But when we actually compare them, we can't know which one is true and which is not, Lessing maintains. And if the truth of religions cannot be told apart from their falsehood, only pride can lead adherents of a religion to believe that "only their God is the true God" and to try to force the "better God upon the whole world for its own good."[34]

What should they do instead of trying to persuade each other of the superior truth of their religion? Here is how Lessing puts his positive point. It comes in the form of a statement addressed to the representatives of Judaism, Christianity, and Islam:

> Let each of you rival the others only in uncorrupted love, free from prejudice. Let each of you strive to show the power of [his religion]. Come to the aid of this power in gentleness, with heartfelt tolerance, in charity, with sincerest submission to God.[35]

To Lessing, religions—or at least the Abrahamic faiths—are enablers of uncorrupted love. The test of their truth is the ability to generate such love, and that's where gift giving comes in. Believers' concern should be to give what others need and delight in, and to leave the question of truth open—to be decided by an impartial judge on the basis of each religion's track record in fostering love.

A child of the Age of Enlightenment—one of the *fathers* of the Enlightenment!—Lessing thought he could neatly separate the practice of love from the question of truth. Truth-claims are disputed, he felt, but we all agree on what is a loving thing to do. Moreover, he also believed that being a Jew, a Christian, or a Muslim is a dispensable addition to a more basic, generic humanness stripped of all the particularities of culture and religion. Like truth, cultural and religious particularities divide; like love, generic humanness unites. For a noble person, it wouldn't matter that he or she is a Jew, a Christian, or a Muslim; it would be "enough . . . to be called a human being."[36]

The problem is that there are no generic human beings and there is no generic love. We know neither what love is nor what it means to be a human being outside of the traditions—mainly religious—in which we were raised and in which we live. There are Jewish ways of being human and of loving; there are Christian ways of being human and of loving; there are Muslim ways of being human and of loving, and so on. The various ways of being human and of loving as presented by differing religions are not identical, though they may significantly overlap.

Put differently, Jewishness and Christianness, for instance, are not garments of humanity and love that can be taken off at will; they are the stuff of a particular humanity and a particular love. And that brings us back to the question of truth. The overarching perspectives on life, with their metaphysical and moral claims to truth, are what give concrete content to what we think "love" or "being human" means. Each one of these religions sees its own vision of what it means to be human as true to who human beings in fact are. Each makes a truth-claim of universal validity. And yet, each makes this claim from a

135

decidedly particular standpoint—and, as a result, all can engage in debates about the very meaning of humanity and of the best ways to live human lives.

On its own, Lessing's exchange of gifts in the practice of "uncorrupted love" is important but insufficient. It needs to be supplemented by the exchange of gifts *in search of truth and mutual understanding.* At the most basic level, the truth-claims of many religions—notably those of the Abrahamic faiths—are contained in their sacred texts. My suggestion is that people of faith should practice "hermeneutical hospitality" in regard to each other's sacred texts and exchange gifts as they do so.[37] Each should enter sympathetically into others' efforts to interpret their sacred texts as well as listen to how others perceive them as readers of their own sacred texts. Such hospitality will not necessarily lead to agreement in the interpretation of each other's respective scriptures. And it will certainly not lead to overall agreement among different religious communities for the simple reason that they hold distinct—even if, in some cases, partly overlapping—texts as authoritative. But such hermeneutical exchanges of gifts will help people of faith to better understand their own and others' sacred texts, to see each other as companions rather than combatants in the struggle for truth, to better respect each other's humanness, and to practice beneficence toward one another.

In Praise of Disagreement

The two forms of gift exchanges—Lessing's beneficence and my hermeneutical hospitality—will not remove all disagreements and all conflict among various religious communities. In fact, removal of disagreements and conflict may not even be desirable. Public life without disagreement and conflict is a utopian dream whose realization under the nonutopian conditions of this world would do more harm than good.[38] But this kind of gift exchange makes it possible to negotiate disagreement and conflict in mutual respect, and it even contributes to a significant measure of convergence and agreement. Religious communities will continue to disagree and argue. The point is to help them argue productively as friends rather than destructively as enemies.

Ongoing arguments are, of course, no substitute for action. There is no exit from acting.[39] Even as we argue, we act. In a democratic polity, one important way in which we act is by voting. We argue, and then we vote, and then we argue again—or at least that's what citizens of well-functioning democracies marked by civility do. There is no reason to think that members of different religious communities could not do the same without having to leave their religion locked up in their hearts, homes, and sanctuaries.

Conclusion

The Cairo Speech

On June 4, 2009, President Obama delivered a speech at the University of Cairo in an attempt to redefine relations between the United States and Muslim communities at the beginning of his presidency. His main theme was the deep tensions between them and the wars in Iraq and Afghanistan. It was a moral and philosophical speech, not merely a political and pragmatic one. In it, he suggested an alternative to the "clash of civilizations."

A conviction that pervades the Cairo speech and indeed carries its whole weight was signaled early on through a brief autobiographical reference:

> I am a Christian, but my father came from a Kenyan family that includes generations of Muslims. As a boy, I spent several years in Indonesia and heard the call of the azaan at the break of dawn and the fall of dusk. As a young man, I worked in Chicago communities where many found dignity and peace in their Muslim faith.[1]

His Christian faith, the president suggests, is not just different from Islam; it includes appreciation for Islam and contains some

139

of the heritage of Islam. His faith identity as a Christian is complex, and it is both like and unlike the faith identity of a Muslim.

As it is with his own experience, so it is with whole communities and nations, President Obama suggested. The consequences of such complex social identities for the relations between the United States and Muslim communities are immense. These relations should not be defined simply by religious and cultural "differences," but by "overlaps" and "common principles" as well. To illustrate the commonalities, at the end of the speech he invoked a rule he described as common to all religions—"that we do unto others as we would have them do unto us."[2] This moral principle, President Obama stated, "transcends nations and peoples"; it is "a belief that isn't new; that isn't black or white or brown; that isn't Christian, or Muslim, or Jew."

In relations between religions, both differences and commonalities count. If we see only differences, we will "empower those who sow hatred rather than peace, and who promote conflict rather than cooperation." If we see only commonalities, we will either have to conform ourselves to others or they will have to conform to us; most likely, we will distort and dishonor both others and ourselves. Only when we see and respect both—undeniable differences that give communities a peculiar character *and* commonalities that bind them together—will we be able to honor each and promote the viable coexistence of all.

President Obama's embrace of both differences and commonalities between religions and civilizations was directed against those who argue that, as he put it, "we are fated to disagree, and civilizations are doomed to clash." He had in mind the followers of Samuel Huntington and his famous thesis about the "clash of civilizations,"[3] which served as the ideological underpinning for President Bush's war on terror. Huntington argued that at the beginning of the twenty-first century, cultures and civilizations with religion at their center have replaced ideologies as the source of self-understanding and identification. Civilizations differ, and civilizational differences matter to people more than similarities. Civilizations are therefore bound to clash.

Huntington's thesis is good for fighting, but not for living together in peace. As he was reaching out to Muslim communities around the world, President Obama suggested replacing the clash of civilizations with a vision of the cooperation of those who are clearly different and yet have much in common. But was that a case of wishful thinking? Are religions capable of such cooperation? Are they capable of sharing the same political space and cooperating for the common good?

Faith and Political Pluralism

If Sayyid Qutb speaks for monotheistic religions—or even for Islam, the second most numerous religion in the world (after Christianity) with over 1.57 billion adherents[4]—then President Obama's pluralistic vision is an expression of wishful thinking. Religious and cultural plurality is the inescapable reality of our globalized world, but as a political project pluralism is then doomed to utter failure. As I have discussed in the introduction, Qutb lines up the beliefs in the one God, in one single political authority, and in one universal moral law—and advocates the use of physical force to establish the rule of the one God and God's law in the world. If Qutb has correctly expressed the inner logic of monotheism, then monotheism is clearly totalitarian. Given that monotheisms are dominant religions in contemporary multireligious and pluralistic societies, the only workable option would then be the secular exclusion of religion from the public realm.

The exclusion of religion from the public realm would clearly entail massive religious suppression, as it is against the religious convictions of many people to keep their faith locked in the

141

privacy of their hearts or its influence restricted to the boundaries of religious communities. But if Qutb correctly expresses the political implications of monotheism, then the alternative to secular exclusion of religion from public life would be totalitarian saturation of public life by a single religion—one religion imposing its own vision of the good life upon all others with an iron fist. So if Qutb is right, the alternatives are either the religious suppression of all religions but one, or the secular suppression of all religions—a manifestly unjust situation in either case.

In this book, I have argued that a plausible interpretation of the Christian faith opposes religious totalitarianism and supports pluralism as a political project. A similar argument can be made, and has been made, from the perspective of other religions as well, including Islam.[5] (To repeat: Qutb's is not *the* Islamic position; indeed, his views have been explicitly condemned by many Muslims and do not represent the mainstream of Islam!) Here is the summary of my argument for pluralism as a political project in contrast to Qutb's religious totalitarianism.

1. All monotheists agree that there is "no god but God." This is not just the basic tenet of Islam; it is the most basic monotheistic conviction. Qutb derives from it a political philosophy best described as religious totalitarianism. I believe that the faith in one God who commands love of neighbor—who enjoins us to treat others as we would want them to treat us—commits us to pluralism as a political project.

2. That God alone is God means for Qutb that all authority of human beings—whether they are priests, politicians, or ordinary people—over others is a form of idolatry. I believe that political authority—or any other authority—need not stand in opposition to God's authority. Critical

for monotheists is not to reject all nondivine authority but to give ultimate allegiance to the one God and to obey nothing contrary to God's commands. In biblical terms, one can hold together the claim that "we must obey God rather than any human authority" (Acts 5:29) and that we should be "subject to the governing authorities" (Rom. 13:1).

3. According to Qutb, guidance as to how to lead one's personal life and how to organize social life comes from God alone. I believe that, though the revelation of God is of critical importance, human understanding of God's revelation is always limited in that human beings—including all interpreters of revelation—are fallible and finite. Moreover, while God's revelation touches all spheres of life, it leaves many important details of life unregulated. Since God is the Creator and therefore the Lord of all reality, there is truth, goodness, and beauty to be found in all cultures, and knowledge of what human beings ought to do can come from many different sources—including the sciences, philosophy, and other religions.

4. Qutb argues that the Muslim community is "the name of a group of people whose manners, ideas and concepts, rules and regulations, values and criteria, are all derived from the Islamic source."[6] Though it is important for faith to shape all spheres of life, I believe that the "manners, ideas and concepts, rules and regulations, values and criteria" that shape a community must be only *compatible* with God's revelation, rather than all being directly derived from God's revelation.

5. In Qutb's view, true followers of God are called to cut themselves off completely from communities that exhibit ignorance of the guidance of God. In my view, true followers of God are called to live in the world and not be

of the world (see Mark 16:15; John 17:14–16). They are to love God above all things and follow Jesus Christ as their Lord; that is their difference from the rest of the world—whether they think and act in the same way, in a similar way, or in a completely different way from others. Christianity is not a "culture" or a "civilization"; it is a way of living centered on Christ *in* many diverse cultures and civilizations.

6. Since God is one and Creator, argues Qutb, the law of God that regulates human personal and social life applies always and everywhere. Though I agree that God's moral laws have universal validity, I believe they may be imposed as the law of the land only through valid democratic processes and not against the will of the people.

7. Qutb writes, "The foremost duty of Islam in this world is to depose *Jahiliyyah* [ignorance of the divine guidance] from the leadership of man, and to take the leadership into its own hands and enforce the particular way of life which is its permanent feature."[7] I believe that Christians have no such duty, and indeed that something like a violent "Christian revolution" would be unjust, unloving, and counterproductive, and in any case profoundly unchristian.

8. According to Qutb, true believers are called to witness to faith that there is "no god but God"—a faith that must be embraced freely since there is no compulsion in religion. I agree that faith must be embraced freely and therefore must be offered to people as a gift, not imposed as a law. Just for that reason, any form of imposition of a social system or of legislation allegedly based on God's revelation must be rejected. To affirm freedom of religion is to reject any form of religious totalitarianism and to embrace pluralism as a political project.

Conclusion

With these eight points I trust that I have sufficiently attended to the problem of faith's coerciveness—at the level of theory, of course, not at the level of practice. The faiths that affirm social pluralism of the kind that I have just sketched can insert themselves as one voice among many into public life to promote their own vision of human flourishing and serve the common good. Even more, as I have suggested in chapter 4, Jews, Christians, and Muslims (as well as adherents of other world religions) have a common mission in the world. It is not just to roll up their sleeves and collaborate in stemming the relentless and rising tide of human misery,[8] whether that comes in the form of disease, hunger, violated rights, or a polluted environment. The common mission is also to make plausible in contemporary culture that human beings will flourish only when the love of pleasure, a dominant driving force in our culture, gives way to the pleasure of love. Different religions will disagree on how the transition from love of pleasure to the pleasure of love can be achieved, and they will not see eye to eye about what a truly pleasurable love concretely means. Yet together they can create a climate in which love of pleasure has been exposed as empty and in which a robust debate is carried on about the most important question of all: "What makes for a life worthy of being called good?"

145

Acknowledgments

I t is not easy to tell the history of this book; therefore the acknowledgements, always inadequate, will be doubly so.

The pivotal event was the invitation to deliver the 2006 Laing Lectures at Regent College, Vancouver, Canada. These lectures comprise its first three chapters. I thank my friends at Regent College, especially John Stackhouse, for the invitation and for stimulating conversations in that beautiful city. I have also presented all three of these lectures individually at various venues. The same is true of the remaining four chapters, even if I wrote each of them originally for a specific occasion. Chapter 4 ("Human Flourishing") I wrote in 2008 for the working group of Jewish and Christian scholars on "Hope and Responsibility for Human Future" organized by the Institute for Theological Inquiry. Chapter 5 ("Identity and Difference") goes back to a lecture I delivered in Bad Urah, Germany, in 1994 at the conference titled "The Gospel in Our Pluralistic Culture," but I revised it massively for this volume. Chapter 6 ("Sharing Wisdom") was a Christian position paper (written in a setting of interfaith discussions with representatives of six world religions) for the third meeting of the Elijah Board of World Religious Leaders, held in 2007 in Amritsar, India. Finally, I first presented the content of chapter 7 ("Public Engagement") at the 2005 conference on New Religious Pluralism and Democracy at Georgetown University. I owe a debt of gratitude to organizers and many participants in these working groups, conferences, and other venues where I delivered these texts as lectures for engaging and improving my work.

I edited all the texts freshly for this volume. My little house on the wooded Island Ugljan, Croatia, overlooking the beautiful Adriatic was a perfect spot to do such work. My sister, Vlasta, my mother, Mira, as well as my cousins Daniela and Mario were kind enough to take care of many domestic duties and keep an eye on my sons, Nathanael and Aaron, so I could be free to write. From the distant New Haven, Ryan McAnnally-Linz has proven himself time and time again as an absolutely first-rate research assistant—efficient, informed, thoughtful, and constructively critical. I am immensely grateful to them all. Bob Hosack and the whole Brazos Press team deserve my thanks for so ably making the book see the light of day, and, yes, for their patience as well.

Finally, I dedicate the book to my friend Skip Masback. He went with me through valleys and climbed on some high peaks. We share a passion for seeing our faith serve human flourishing and the common good.

Notes

Introduction

1. Mark Lilla, *The Stillborn God: Religion, Politics, and the Modern West* (New York: Knopf, 2007), 309.

2. Just for the record: religious totalitarianism is not the only form of totalitarianism. Indeed, all of the most bloodthirsty forms of totalitarianism over the past century or so—Nazism, Stalinism, Maoism—were not religious in character at all.

3. On Qutb, see John L. Esposito, *The Future of Islam* (Oxford: Oxford University Press, 2010), 67–68.

4. On Christian Reconstructionism, see John Pottenger, *Reaping the Whirlwind: Liberal Democracy and the Religious Axis* (Washington, DC: Georgetown University Press, 2007), 208–39.

5. For Islamic arguments for political pluralism, see Feisal Abdul Rauf, *What's Right with Islam: A New Vision for Muslims and the West* (New York: Harper-Collins, 2004).

6. Sayyid Qutb, *Milestones* (Chicago: Kazi, 2007), 90.

7. Ibid., 2.

8. Ibid., 14.

9. Ibid., 89.

10. At the end of *Milestones* Qutb underscores that the fundamental struggle in the world today is a religious one, not economic, political, or cultural. "The struggle between the Believers and their enemies is in essence a struggle of belief, and not in any way of anything else. The enemies are angered only because of their faith, enraged only because of their belief. This was not a political or an economic or a racial struggle; had it been any of these, its settlement would have been easy, the solution of its difficulties would have been simple. But essentially it was a struggle between beliefs—either unbelief or faith, either *Jahiliyyah* or Islam" (ibid., 110).

11. Ibid., 81.

149

12. One example from Christianity would be Thomas Müntzer, one of the leaders of the German Peasant War in 1525.

13. H. Richard Niebuhr, *Christ and Culture* (1956; repr., New York: HarperCollins, 2001).

14. On the relationship between religious exclusivism on the part of Christians and Muslims and the embrace of pluralism as a political project, see Miroslav Volf, *Allah: A Christian Response* (San Francisco: HarperOne, 2011), chap. 12.

Chapter 1 Malfunctions of Faith

1. See Friedrich Nietzsche, *Twilight of the Idols and The Anti-Christ*, ed. Michael Tanner, trans. R. J. Hollingdale (1888; repr. London: Penguin, 2003).

2. Ibid., 128.

3. For such an argument, see Pope John Paul II, *Evangelium vitae* (1995), http://www.vatican.va/edocs/ENG0141/_INDEX.HTM.

4. For such an argument, see Alexander Sanger, *Beyond Choice: Reproductive Freedom in the 21st Century* (New York: PublicAffairs, 2004).

5. For the distinction, see Friedrich Heiler's *Prayer: A Study in the History and Psychology of Religion* (1932; repr., Oxford: Oneworld, 1997), chap. 6.

6. Muhammad Iqbal, *The Reconstruction of Religious Thought in Islam* (Lahore: Sang-E-Meel, 1996), 111.

7. See *Engaged Buddhism: Buddhist Liberation Movements in Asia*, ed. Christopher S. Queen and Sallie B. King (Albany: State University of New York Press, 1996).

8. Friedrich Nietzsche, *The Gay Science*, trans. Walter Kaufmann (New York: Vintage, 1974), 182.

9. On idolatry as substitution, see Moshe Halbertal and Avishai Margalit, *Idolatry*, trans. Naomi Goldbloom (Cambridge, MA: Harvard University Press, 1992), 40–44.

10. See Joel Osteen, *Become a Better You: 7 Keys to Improving Your Life Every Day* (New York: Free Press, 2007), 37.

11. See Thomas Aquinas, *Summa Theologiae* IaIIae.71.5, 72.6.

12. Max Weber, *The Protestant Ethic and the Spirit of Capitalism*, trans. Talcott Parsons (1905; repr., London: Routledge, 2002), 123. See also Miroslav Volf, *Captive to the Word of God: Engaging Scripture for Theological Reflection* (Grand Rapids: Eerdmans, 2010), chap. 5.

13. Zygmunt Bauman, *Life in Fragments: Essays in Postmodern Morality* (Oxford: Blackwell, 1995), 259–62.

14. For fascinating, if controversial, studies of the human tendencies to obey orders and fill social roles, see Stanley Milgram, *Obedience to Authority: An Experimental View* (New York: Harper & Row, 1974), and Philip Zimbardo, "The Power and Pathology of Imprisonment," Cong. Rec. 15 (October 25, 1971).

15. For an argument that when faith in the true God is lost, it is not atheism that follows but a kind of polytheism, see H. Richard Niebuhr, *Radical Monotheism and Western Culture with Supplementary Essays* (London: Faber and Faber, 1960), 31–38, 95–96.

16. See Christian Scharen, *Faith as a Way of Life: A Vision for Pastoral Leadership* (Grand Rapids: Eerdmans, 2008), 14–26.

17. Karl Marx, "Towards a Critique of Hegel's *Philosophy of Right*," in *Karl Marx: Selected Writings*, ed. David McLellan (Oxford: Oxford University Press, 2000), 72.

18. See Nicholas Wolterstorff, "The Role of Religion in Decision and Discussion of Political Issues," in *Religion in the Public Square: The Place of Religious Convictions in Political Debate*, ed. Robert Audi and Nicholas Wolterstorff (Lanham, MD: Rowman & Littlefield, 1997), 67–120.

19. For a critique of the claim that Muslims believe in a different god than Christians (and that they therefore inhabit a different moral universe with the result that we must fight them rather than morally persuade or negotiate with them), see Volf, *Allah*.

20. Sam Harris, *The End of Faith: Religion, Terror, and the Future of Reason* (New York: W. W. Norton, 2004), 23.

21. See Plato, *Crito* 49a–e.

Chapter 2 Idleness

1. See Claus Westermann, *Genesis 1–11: A Continental Commentary*, trans. John J. Scullion (Minneapolis: Fortress, 1994), 139–46; Claus Westermann, *Blessing in the Bible and the Life of the Church*, trans. Keith Crim (Philadelphia: Fortress, 1978), 59.

2. See, for example, the popular book by Rhonda Byrne, *The Secret* (New York: Atria, 2006), and its sequel, *The Power* (New York: Atria, 2010).

3. See Miroslav Volf, *Free of Charge: Giving and Forgiving in a Culture Stripped of Grace* (Grand Rapids: Zondervan, 2006), chap. 1.

4. See Olive Wyon, *The School of Prayer* (Philadelphia: Westminster, 1944), 28–35.

5. For a discussion of this tradition, see Walter Brueggemann, *Theology of the Old Testament: Testimony, Dispute, Advocacy* (Minneapolis: Fortress, 1997), 173–81. On the importance of the distinction between deliverance and blessing, see Westermann, *Blessing*, 1–23.

6. Immanuel Kant, *Critique of Practical Reason*, trans. Mary Gregor (Cambridge: Cambridge University Press, 1997), 5.122–34.

7. See Miroslav Volf, *Work in the Spirit: Toward a Theology of Work* (Oxford: Oxford University Press, 1991), 97.

8. See also Miroslav Volf, *The End of Memory: Remembering Rightly in a Violent World* (Grand Rapids: Eerdmans, 2006), 78–81.

9. According to Augustine's famous statement, our hearts are restless until they find their rest in God (see Augustine, *Confessions* 1.1.1).

10. On the discussion of how work relates to each person's specific gifts and callings, see Volf, *Work in the Spirit*. There I develop a theology of work that is based not on a general calling of God that is then made specific by the place of a person within a social system, but on specific gifts (combined with callings) that God gives to each individual. This opens up a possibility of a much more dynamic understanding of human work.

11. Church fathers engaged in intense reflection as to what kind of work is permissible for a Christian to undertake. Tertullian, for example, reflected on both

the profession of a soldier and a variety of activities associated with the crafting of idols (see Tertullian, *On Idolatry* 4–10, 19, available at http://www.ccel.org/ccel /schaff/anf03.iv.iv.ii.html). More recently, Karl Barth also discussed what kind of work is permissible for a Christian to do; see Karl Barth, *Church Dogmatics* III/4, ed. G. W. Bromiley and T. F. Torrance (Edinburgh: T&T Clark, 1961), 527–34. We need to renew such reflection today, and connect it with morally appropriate ends, including protecting human dignity and ensuring sustainability.

12. On this distinction, see Gregory M. Reichberg, "Jus ad Bellum," and Nicholas Rengger, "The Jus in Bello in Historical and Philosophical Perspective," in *War: Essays in Political Philosophy*, ed. Larry May (Cambridge: Cambridge University Press, 2008), 11–46.

13. For further discussion, see chap. 4.

14. Lewis Carroll, *Through the Looking Glass* (London: Macmillan, 1871), 46. On this, especially as it comes to expression in Ecclesiastes, see Miroslav Volf, *Captive to the Word of God: Engaging Scripture for Theological Reflection* (Grand Rapids: Eerdmans, 2010), chap. 5.

15. For a moving discussion of the transitoriness of all human efforts, see Alexander Schmemann, *The Eucharist: The Sacrament of the Kingdom*, trans. Paul Kachur (Crestwood, NY: St. Vladimir's Seminary Press, 1988), 127.

16. See John Paul II, *Laborem exercens* (1981), http://www.vatican.va/edocs /ENG0217/_INDEX.HTM; Volf, *Work in the Spirit*, 98–102.

17. For further discussion, see Volf, *Work in the Spirit*, 96–98.

Chapter 3 Coerciveness

1. Douglas Johnston and Cynthia Sampson, *Religion, the Missing Dimension of Statecraft* (New York: Oxford University Press, 1994).

2. Mark Jurgensmeyer, *Terror in the Mind of God: The Global Rise of Religious Violence* (Berkeley: University of California Press, 2000).

3. Scott R. Appleby, *The Ambivalence of the Sacred: Religion, Violence, and Reconciliation* (Lanham, MD: Rowman & Littlefield, 1999), 2. A secularizing impact of the wars of religion was felt even as far afield from everyday concerns as theories of knowledge are sometimes deemed to be. As Stephen Toulmin has argued in *Cosmopolis*, modernity did not emerge, as often claimed, simply as a result of its protagonists' endeavor to dispel the darkness of tradition and superstition with the light of philosophical and scientific reason. It was not accidental that Descartes "discovered" the one correct method to acquire knowledge in a time when "over much of the continent . . . people had a fair chance of having their throats cut and their houses burned down by strangers who merely disliked their religion" (Stephen Toulmin, *Cosmopolis: The Hidden Agenda of Modernity* [New York: Free Press, 1990], 17). A new way of establishing truth "that was independent of, and neutral between, particular religious loyalties" seemed an attractive alternative to war fueled by dogmatic claims (ibid., 70).

4. For an alternative interpretation of the "wars of religion," see William T. Cavanaugh, *The Myth of Religious Violence: Secular Ideology and the Roots of Modern Conflict* (Oxford: Oxford University Press, 2009), 123–80.

5. For a survey, see Gottfried Maron, "Frieden und Krieg: Ein Blick in die Theologie- und Kirchengeschichte," in *Glaubenskriege in Vergangenheit und Gegenwart*, ed. Peter Herrmann (Goettingen: Vandenhoeck und Ruprecht, 1996), 17–35. See also Karlheinz Deschner, *Kriminalgeschichte des Christentums*, 9 vols. (Reinbeck: Rowohlt, 1986–) and a response to his work: H. R. Seeliger, ed., *Kriminalizierung des Christentums? Karlheinz Deschners Kirchengeschichte auf dem Pruefstand* (Freiburg: Herder, 1993).

6. The best way to explain my use of "thick" and "thin" is to compare it with usage by others. Clifford Geertz has made the use of the contrasting pair "thick" and "thin" popular in his *Interpretation of Cultures* (New York: Basic Books, 1974), 3–30. He himself has taken it over from Gilbert Ryle. Both use the term in the syntagma "thick or thin *description*" of the same phenomenon. The typical case of "thin" description is "rapidly contracting his right eyelid" and of the "thick" description, "practicing burlesque of a friend faking a wink to deceive an innocent into thinking a conspiracy is in motion." In his book *Thick and Thin: Moral Argument at Home and Abroad* (Notre Dame: University of Notre Dame Press, 1994), Michael Walzer has introduced an altered sense of "thick" and "thin" as he applies them to moral arguments. He writes, "It is not my claim to offer a thick description of moral argument, rather to point to a kind of argument that is itself 'thick'—richly referential, culturally resonant, locked into a locally established symbolic system or network of meaning. 'Thin' is simply a contrasting term" (xi n1). (For a more recent and still different use of "thick" and "thin," where these designations refer to "the two types of human relations," and where "thick relations are in general our relations to the near and dear" and "thin relations are in general our relations to the stranger and the remote," see Avishai Margalit, *The Ethics of Memory* [Cambridge, MA: Harvard University Press, 2002], 7, 37–40.) My use is similar to Walzer's, in that, just as Walzer claims the case in relation to morality, one arrives at the "thin" understanding and practice of the faith by abstraction from the "thick" understanding and practice. "Thick" for me is, for instance, a worshiper who expresses a conviction that God is triune, and understands this conviction to be governed by the story of Jesus Christ and to imply an obligation to act in certain ways; "thin" is the flashing of three fingers on the part of Serbian soldiers in what looks like a victory sign, but is in fact a sign of a trinitarian faith reduced by that very act to no more than an empty marker of cultural difference. Or, to give an example from the United States, "thin" is when the words "under God" in the Pledge of Allegiance are drained of specific religious content so that they become more of a cultural tradition than a theological assertion; "thick" is when "God" in the said phrase refers to the God of Jesus Christ or to Allah of the Qur'an or to Yahweh of the Hebrew Bible, which might make the phrase unconstitutional under the "no establishment" clause (see the editorial "Taking on the Pledge," *Christian Century*, July 17–30, 2002, 5). Though our usage is analogous, Walzer's and my concerns are, however, different. I am concerned to show how the "thinning" of religious practice opens religious convictions to be misused to legitimize violence because it strips away precisely what in "thick" religious faith guards against such misuse, whereas Walzer's concern is to show that morality is "thick" from the beginning and that the "thin" morality as universal always resides within the "thick" as particular (Walzer, *Thick and Thin*, 4).

7. See Miroslav Volf, *Exclusion and Embrace: A Theological Exploration of Identity, Otherness, and Reconciliation* (Nashville: Abingdon, 1996).

8. There are other arguments for the same thesis as well, some of which I will address indirectly. One argument for the violent character of Christianity claims that religions are by nature violent, and that the Christian faith, being a religion, is therefore also by nature violent. Jurgensmeyer's *Terror in the Mind of God* rests on such a reading of religion. A central reason why violence has accompanied religion's renewed political presence, he argues, has to do with "the nature of religious imagination, which always has had the propensity to absolutize and to project images of cosmic war" (242). Cosmic war is waged not for its own sake but for the sake of peace, of course. Precisely as a phenomenon at whose core lies cosmic war, religion has been "order restoring and life affirming" (159). But if in its pursuit of peace religion is not to leave a trail of blood and tears, it cannot be left to its own devices. It needs "the temper of rationality and fair play that Enlightenment values give to civil society" (243). Religion qua religion is violent. To have a socially positive role, it needs to be redeemed by Enlightenment values.

The argument that a religion that counts among its great teachers Augustine, Thomas Aquinas, and Luther (to name just a few great theological minds) would need to learn to be "rational" from Enlightenment thinkers betrays a rather narrow understanding of "rationality." But at least such an account of rationality is plausible. Implausible, however, is the claim that a religion that counts St. Francis among its greatest saints does not have resources of its own to learn about fair play but must borrow them from Enlightenment thinkers. The pressure to make such implausible claims comes from "thinning" Christian convictions to generic religious beliefs and then placing images of cosmic war at the heart of these. In the process, everything specific to the Christian faith has been lost.

9. Regina Schwartz, *The Curse of Cain: The Violent Legacy of Monotheism* (Chicago: University of Chicago Press, 1997), 63.

10. See Jan Assmann, *Moses the Egyptian: The Memory of Egypt in Western Monotheism* (Cambridge, MA: Harvard University Press, 1997).

11. Željko Mardešić (Jakov Jukić), *Lica i maske svetoga: Ogledi iz društvene religiologije* ("Faces and Masks of the Holy") (Zagreb: Kršćanska Sadašnjost, 1997), 242–44.

12. For a critique of Schwartz along these lines, see Miroslav Volf, "Jehovah on Trial," *Christianity Today*, April 27, 1998, 32–35.

13. For the following, see Miroslav Volf, "'The Trinity is Our Social Program': The Doctrine of the Trinity and the Shape of Social Engagement," *Modern Theology* 14 (1998): 403–23.

14. In *Allah*, I have made an argument that the belief in one God who commands love of neighbor—to treat others as you want them to treat you—in fact, under certain conditions, leads to embracing pluralism as a political project (see chap. 12).

15. Rosemary Radford Ruether, *Sexism and God-Talk: Toward a Feminist Theology* (Boston: Beacon, 1983), 77.

16. Rowan Williams, *On Christian Theology* (Oxford: Blackwell, 2000), 68.

17. Ibid., 68–69.

18. See John Milbank, *Theology and Social Theory: Beyond Secular Reason* (Oxford: Blackwell, 1990).

19. Jacques Derrida, *Spectres of Marx: The State of the Debt, the Work of Mourning, and the New International*, trans. Peggy Kamuf (New York: Routledge, 1994), 75.

20. John Caputo, *The Prayers and Tears of Jacques Derrida: Religion without Religion* (Bloomington: Indiana University Press, 1997), 74.

21. Derrida, *Spectres of Marx*, 90.

22. See Friedrich Nietzsche, *Thus Spoke Zarathustra*, in *The Portable Nietzsche*, trans. Walter Kaufmann (New York: Penguin, 1954), 139, 253.

23. On the relationship between conditionality and unconditionality, see Volf, *Exclusion and Embrace*, 215–16.

24. See Richard B. Hays, *The Moral Vision of the New Testament: Community, Cross, New Creation* (San Francisco: HarperSanFrancisco, 1996), 175.

25. See Richard Bauckham, *The Theology of the Book of Revelation* (Cambridge: Cambridge University Press, 1993), 74, 90.

26. On the important distinction between hope for and belief in universal salvation, see Hans Urs von Balthasar, *Dare We Hope That All Men Will Be Saved?* trans. David Kipp and Lothar Krauth (San Francisco: Ignatius, 1988).

27. See Volf, *Exclusion and Embrace*, 275–306.

28. Appleby, *Ambivalence of the Sacred*, 16.

29. Michael Sells's account of religion's relation to genocide in Bosnia (*The Bridge Betrayed: Religion and Genocide in Bosnia* [Berkeley: University of California Press, 1996]) rests on an extremely "thin" account of the Christian faith; it functions more like a cultural resource with little connection to its origins than as a living faith committed to the sacred Scriptures and the best of the tradition. The "thinning" was, of course, not undertaken by him, but by people he studied.

30. Margalit, *Ethics of Memory*, 100.

31. Personal communication.

32. See John Milbank, *Being Reconciled: Ontology and Pardon* (London: Routledge, 2003), 28–37, for a discussion of the violence entailed in watching violence.

Chapter 4 Human Flourishing

1. Josef Pieper, *Hope and History: Five Salzburg Lectures*, trans. David Kipp (San Francisco: Ignatius, 1994), 20.

2. Jürgen Moltmann, *Theology of Hope: On the Ground and the Implications of a Christian Eschatology*, trans. Margaret Kohl (San Francisco: HarperSanFrancisco, 1991). For a brief summary, see also Jürgen Moltmann, *The Coming of God: On Christian Eschatology*, trans. Margaret Kohl (Minneapolis: Fortress, 1996), 25.

3. See Philip Rieff, *The Triumph of the Therapeutic: Uses of Faith after Freud* (New York: Harper & Row, 1966), 232–61.

4. Augustine, *Trinity* 13.10.

5. Ibid., 13.8.

6. Augustine, *City of God* 19.17.

7. Charles Taylor, *A Secular Age* (Cambridge, MA: Harvard University Press, 2007), 245.

8. Karl Marx, *Critique of the Gotha Program*, in *Essential Writings of Karl Marx* (St. Petersburg, FL: Red and Black, 2010), 243.

9. Andrew Delbanco, *The Real American Dream: A Meditation on Hope* (Cambridge, MA: Harvard University Press, 1999), 77.

10. The claim that the scope of hope was reduced when it was directed away from God and toward the nation has been contested. Delbanco himself maintains that the national ideal is lesser than God. In his review of Delbanco's book, Richard Rorty protests, "Why, one can imagine Whitman asking, should we Americans take God's word for it that he is more vast than the free, just, utopian nation of our dreams? Whitman famously called the United States of America 'the greatest poem.' He took narratives that featured God to be lesser poems—useful in their day, because suitable for the needs of a younger humanity. But now we are more grown up" (Richard Rorty, "I Hear America Sighing," *New York Times Book Review*, November 7, 1999, 16). The dispute about which dream is bigger—the dream of a nation or of God—must be decided in conjunction with the question of whether God in fact exists. For only under the assumption of God's nonexistence can God be declared lesser than the nation, however conceived.

11. Herman Melville, *White Jacket; Or, the World in a Man-of-War* (1850; repr., New York: Plume, 1979), chap. 36.

12. Delbanco, *Real American Dream*, 96, 103.

13. Ibid., 103.

14. Michael Oakeshott, "Political Education," in Michael Oakeshott, *Rationalism in Politics and Other Essays* (Indianapolis: Liberty, 1991), 48.

15. Offering a particularly bleak version of this point, Arthur Schopenhauer writes that in human existence, there is only "momentary gratification, fleeting pleasure conditioned by wants, much and long suffering, constant struggle, *bellum omnium*, everything a hunter and everything hunted, pressure, want, need and anxiety, shrieking and howling, and this goes on in *secula seculorum* or until once again the crust of the planet breaks" (*The World as Will and Representation*, trans. E. F. J. Payne [Mineola, NY: Dover, 1969], 2:354).

16. Shakespeare, *Merchant of Venice* 2.6.12–13.

17. This observation fits with one of the central conclusions of the Grand Study—a study of well-adjusted Harvard sophomores begun in 1937, which, after more than seventy years of following its subjects, remains one of "the longest running, and probably most exhaustive, longitudinal studies of mental and physical well-being in history." In an interview in 2008, its longtime director, George Valliant, was asked, "What have you learned from Grand Study men?" His response was that "the only thing that really matters in life are your relationships with other people" (Joshua Wolf Shenk, "What Makes Us Happy?" *The Atlantic*, June 2009, 36). Applied to the question of satisfaction, this suggests that relationships give meaning to pleasure; pleasure hollows itself out without them.

18. Delbanco, *Real American Dream*, 103.

19. Abu Hamid Muhammad al-Ghazali, *The Alchemy of Happiness*, trans. Claud Field (Gloucester: Dodo, 2008), xii.

20. Moses Maimonides, *The Guide of the Perplexed*, trans. Shlomo Pines (Chicago: University of Chicago Press, 1963), 1.2.

21. Ibid., 3.51.

22. Ibid., 3.54. Though prevalent, this "intellectualist" reading of Maimonides's account of human perfection has not remained unchallenged. For an alternative reading that emphasizes not just human apprehension of God but human love of God as well as human "return" to the world as a being transformed by the knowledge of God "to participate in the governance of one's society according to the principles of loving-kindness, righteousness, and judgment," see Menachem Kellner, "Is Maimonides's Ideal Person Austerely Rationalist?" *American Catholic Philosophical Quarterly* 76 (2002): 125–43 (quotation on 134).

23. It has been a widespread Christian *critique* of Islam in the Middle Ages and Renaissance that it is "founded on pleasure," as Pope Pius II expresses in his letter to the Ottoman sultan Mehmed II. See Aeneas Silvius Piccolomini, *Epistola ad Mahomatem II* ("Epistle to Mohammed II"), ed. and trans. Altert R. Baca (New York: Peter Lang, 1990), 91.

24. Anthony T. Kronman, *Education's End: Why Our Colleges and Universities Have Given Up on the Meaning of Life* (New Haven: Yale University Press, 2007).

25. Ibid., 197.

26. See al-Ghazali, *Alchemy of Happiness*, 1–26.

27. See Katerina Ierodiakonou, "The Study of Stoicism: Its Decline and Revival," in *Topics in Stoic Philosophy*, ed. Katerina Ierodiakonou (Oxford: Oxford University Press, 1999), 1–22.

28. For the purposes of this essay, I am following the discussion of Seneca and Stoics in Nicholas Wolterstorff, *Justice: Right and Wrongs* (Princeton: Princeton University Press, 2008), 146–79.

29. See Friedrich Nietzsche, *Beyond Good and Evil* (New York: Vintage, 1989), 15.

30. Friedrich Nietzsche, *On the Genealogy of Morality*, ed. Keith Ansell-Pearson, trans. Carol Diethe (Cambridge: Cambridge University Press, 1994), 8.

31. This last point stands even if it is true that Nietzsche cannot give rational reasons for preferring his noble morality to Western slave morality, because he did not believe that there are objective facts about what is morally right and what is morally wrong. See Brian Leiter, "Nietzsche's Moral and Political Philosophy," *Stanford Encyclopedia of Philosophy*, April 24, 2010, http://plato.stanford.edu/entries/nietzsche-moral-political/.

32. On God as "Divine Butler" and "Cosmic Therapist" among American teenagers, see Christian Smith, *Soul Searching: The Religious and Spiritual Lives of American Teenagers* (Oxford: Oxford University Press, 2005), 165.

33. Terry Eagleton, "Culture and Barbarism: Metaphysics in a Time of Terrorism," *Commonweal*, March 27, 2009, 9.

34. Terry Eagleton, *The Meaning of Life: A Very Short Introduction* (Oxford: Oxford University Press, 2007), 35. For a parallel critique of the impact of postmodernism on the engagement with the question of the meaning of life in educational institutions of higher learning, see Kronman, *Education's End*, 180–94.

35. On this line of interpretation of Augustine, see Oliver O'Donovan, *The Problem of Self-Love in St. Augustine* (New Haven: Yale University Press, 1980), and Wolterstorff, *Justice*, 180–206.

36. I owe the idea that human flourishing consists formally in a combination of life being lived well and life going well to Wolterstorff, *Justice*, 221.

37. Augustine, *Sermon 100 (150)* 7.

Chapter 5 Identity and Difference

1. This chapter has affinities with James Davison Hunter's *To Change the World: The Irony, Tragedy, and Possibility of Christianity in the Late Modern World* (Oxford: Oxford University Press, 2010). The chapter is based on texts I wrote in the mid-1990s: "Soft Difference: Theological Reflections on the Relation between Church and Culture in 1 Peter," *Ex Auditu* 10 (1994): 15–30 (repr., Volf, *Captive to the Word of God*, chap. 2); "Christliche Identität und Differenz: Zur Eigenart der christlichen Präsenz in den modernen Gesellschaften," *Zeitschrift für Theologie und Kirche* 3 (1995): 357–75; and "When Gospel and Culture Intersect: Notes on the Nature of Christian Difference," in *Pentecostalism in Context: Essays in Honor of William W. Menzies*, ed. Wonsuk Ma and Robert P. Menzies (Sheffield: Sheffield Academic Press, 1997), 223–36.

2. Max Weber, "The Protestant Sects and the Spirit of Capitalism," in *From Max Weber: Essays in Sociology*, ed. H. H. Gerth and C. Wright Mills (1948; repr., New York: Routledge, 1998), 305.

3. See Niklas Luhman, *Funktion der Religion* (Frankfurt: Suhrkamp, 1977), 236.

4. See Peter Berger, *The Heretical Imperative: Contemporary Possibilities of Religious Affirmation* (Garden City, NY: Anchor, 1979), 11–17, 26–32.

5. It is inadequate to describe the choice to join a particular religious group as being strictly analogous to the choices people make in the marketplace (so, against Hans Joas, *Do We Need Religion? On the Experience of Self-Transcendence*, trans. Alex Skinner [Boulder: Paradigm, 2008], 28–29).

6. Max Weber, "The Social Psychology of the World Religions," in Gerth and Mills, *From Max Weber*, 288.

7. See Fredrick Barth's introduction to his edited volume *Ethnic Groups and Boundaries: The Social Organization of Culture Difference* (1969; repr., Long Grove, IL: Waveland, 1998).

8. See Anthony P. Cohen, *The Symbolic Construction of Community* (London: Routledge, 1985); Alan Wolfe, "Democracy Versus Sociology: Boundaries and Their Political Consequences," in *Cultivating Differences: Symbolic Boundaries and the Making of Inequality*, ed. Michèle Lamont and Marcel Fournier (Chicago: University of Chicago Press, 1992), 309–25.

9. Ernst Troeltsch, *The Social Teaching of the Christian Churches*, trans. Olive Wyon (1911; repr., Chicago: University of Chicago Press, 1981), 1:331–43.

10. See John Howard Yoder's critique of H. Richard Niebuhr's description of the "Christ against Culture" type of relation between Christianity and culture, which is quite close to Troeltsch's "sect" in John Howard Yoder, "How H. Richard Niebuhr Reasoned: A Critique of *Christ and Culture*," in Glen H. Stassen, D. M. Yeager, and John Howard Yoder, *Authentic Transformation: A New Vision of Christ and Culture* (Nashville: Abingdon, 1996), 31–90.

11. Some sociologists have argued that pluralism leads to the erosion of belief: see Peter Berger, *A Far Glory: The Quest for Faith in an Age of Credulity* (New York: Free Press, 1994); similarly, Hunter, *To Change the World*, 203. As José Casanova has pointed out to me in private conversations, India and the United States are good examples to the contrary. For a critique of Berger's position, see Joas, *Do We Need Religion?* 21–35.

12. See Troeltsch, *Social Teaching*, 1:335, 344.

13. For a discussion of functional differentiation from a theological angle, see Michael Welker, *God's Spirit*, trans. John F. Hoffmeyer (Minneapolis: Augsburg Fortress, 1994), 29–31.

14. See Anthony Giddens, *Runaway World: How Globalization Is Reshaping Our Lives* (New York: Routledge, 2003).

15. So Heidi Campbell, assistant professor in the Department of Communications of Texas A&M University, in personal correspondence (October 23, 2010).

16. Later on I will highlight significant theological reasons for pursuing limited change.

17. See Berger, *Far Glory*, 3–24.

18. Stanley Hauerwas and William H. Willimon, *Resident Aliens: Life in the Christian Colony* (Nashville: Abingdon, 1989), 27.

19. Nicholas Wolterstorff, *What New Haven and Grand Rapids Have to Say to Each Other* (Grand Rapids: Calvin College and Calvin Theological Seminary, 1993), 2.

20. George Lindbeck, "Scripture, Consensus, and Community," in *Biblical Interpretation in Crisis: The Ratzinger Conference on Bible and Church*, ed. Richard John Neuhaus (Grand Rapids: Eerdmans, 1989), 74–101; George Lindbeck, *The Nature of Doctrine: Religion and Theology in a Postliberal Age* (Louisville: Westminster John Knox, 1984).

21. Wolterstorff, *New Haven and Grand Rapids*, 45.

22. This is the point of Hans Frei's preference for "ad hoc correlation." See Hans Frei, *Types of Christian Theology* (New Haven: Yale University Press, 1992), 70–91.

23. Granted, the account of the very center of the Christian faith is bound to change as well, as it has changed over the centuries, even if its fundamentals have remained the same (as enshrined in historic creeds, such as the Nicene or Chalcedonian). Bound by the biblical story and guided by the great creeds and confessions, Christians will keep testing, and possibly revising, how they understand God's revelation in light of what transpires in the world—in the sciences as well as in other religions (see William Stacey Johnson, *The Mystery of God: Karl Barth and the Foundations of Postmodern Theology* [Louisville: Westminster John Knox, 1997]).

24. Dietrich Bonhoeffer, *Discipleship*, ed. Geffrey B. Kelly and John D. Godsey, trans. Barbara Green and Reinhard Krauss (Minneapolis: Fortress, 2001), 259. See also Ernst Feil, *Die Theologie Dietrich Bonhoeffers: Hermeneutik, Christologie, Weltverständniss* (München: Kaiser, 1971), 223–32.

25. Bonhoeffer, *Discipleship*, 250–51.

26. Ibid., 251, quoting a hymn by Christian Friedrich Richter.

27. Michel de Certeau, *The Practice of Everyday Life*, trans. Steven Rendall (Berkeley: University of California Press, 1984), xiv.

28. Ibid., 32.

29. Karl Marx, *Grundrisse: Foundations of the Critique of Political Economy*, trans. Martin Nicolaus (London: Penguin, 1973), 92.

30. Paul Bloom has argued that pleasure is not simply a function of the physical features of the object from which we derive pleasure but also of our own perception and interpretation of that object. See Paul Bloom, *How Pleasure Works: The*

New Science of Why We Like What We Like (New York: W. W. Norton, 2010). The same holds true, I would argue, for at least some forms of pain, hunger being one of them.

31. See Georg W. F. Hegel, *Phenomenology of Spirit*, trans. A. V. Miller (Oxford: Oxford University Press, 1977), 4.184.

32. On modernity as an attempt to reconstruct cultural and intellectual life from the ground up, see Toulmin, *Cosmopolis*.

33. For a critique of apocalypticism which entails identifying "our own expectations for the future with God's plan," see Charles Mathewes, *A Theology of Public Life* (Cambridge: Cambridge University Press, 2007), 38–42, 205–8.

34. Ludwig Wittgenstein, *Philosophical Investigations*, trans. G. E. M. Anscombe (New York: Macmillan, 1973), 8.

35. See Volf, *Exclusion and Embrace*, 65–66.

Chapter 6 Sharing Wisdom

1. Delbanco, *Real American Dream.*

2. See Jonathan Fox, "Religion and State Failure," *International Political Science Review* 25 (2004): 55–76; Jonathan Fox, "The Rise of Religious Nationalism and Conflict," *Journal of Peace Research* 41 (2004): 715–31; David Herbert and John Wolffe, "Religion and Contemporary Conflict in Historical Perspective," in *Religion in History: Conflict, Conversion, and Coexistence*, ed. John Wolffe (Manchester: Manchester University Press, 2004), 286–320.

3. For a recent and compelling book on Christian wisdom, see David F. Ford, *Christian Wisdom: Desiring God and Learning in Love* (Cambridge: Cambridge University Press, 2007).

4. On Christian faith as a way of life, see Miroslav Volf, *Against the Tide: Love in a Time of Petty Dreams and Persisting Enmities* (Grand Rapids: Eerdmans, 2010), 82–85. See also Scharen, *Faith as a Way of Life*. Many Muslims see Islam as a way of life. Obviously, Christians and Muslims mean rather different things by a way of life, and within each religion, extremists, such as Sayyid Qutb, whose account of Islam as a way of life I discuss in the introduction, mean partly different things than those faithful to the classical tradition in each religion. And yet most Muslims and Christians agree: their "religion" is not merely a set of convictions or a set of rituals but a way of living in the world today. Interestingly enough, the phrase "way of life," emptied of its deeper meaning, comes up even in the rhetoric of Western politicians in their legitimate opposition to radical Islam. They see it as a threat to "our way of life" (see President George W. Bush's address to a joint session of Congress from September 20, 2001, available at http://www.washingtonpost.com /wp-srv/nation/specials/attacked/transcripts/bushaddress_092001.html).

5. See Jan Assmann, *Die Mosaische Unterscheidung: Oder der Preis des Monotheismus* (Munich: Carl Hanser, 2003), and Assmann, *Moses the Egyptian.*

6. On the "great commission," see David J. Bosch, "The Structure of Mission," in *Exploring Church Growth*, ed. Wilbert R. Shenk (Grand Rapids: Eerdmans, 1983), 218–48; Peter T. O'Brien, "The Great Commission of Matthew 28:18–20," *Reformed Theological Review* 35 (1976): 66–78; Tom Wright, *Matthew for Everyone: Part Two* (Louisville: Westminster John Knox, 2004), 204–6.

7. On the "great commandment" as motivation for sharing, see Augustine, *On Christian Doctrine* 1.26, 27–29, 30; Augustine, *Letter 130* 14.

8. See William Carey, *An Enquiry into the Obligations of Christians to Use Means for the Conversion of the Heathens* (Leicester: Ann Ireland, 1792).

9. See Catherine Cookson, ed., *The Encyclopedia of Religious Freedom* (London: Routledge, 2003). The U.S. Commission on International Religious Freedom publishes an annual report assessing the global state of religious freedom and persecution. See http://www.uscirf.gov.

10. On noncompetitive forms of giving, see Kathryn Tanner, *Jesus, Humanity, and the Trinity: A Brief Systematic Theology* (Minneapolis: Fortress, 2001), 90–94.

11. On the day of Pentecost as the birth of the church, see Jürgen Moltmann, *The Church in the Power of the Spirit: A Contribution to Messianic Ecclesiology* (Minneapolis: Fortress, 1993).

12. The most egregious example is the conquest of the Americas. See Bartolomé de las Casas, *The Devastation of the Indies: A Brief Account*, trans. Herma Briffault (Baltimore: Johns Hopkins University Press, 1992); George E. Tinker, *Missionary Conquest: The Gospel and Native American Cultural Genocide* (Minneapolis: Augsburg Fortress, 1993); Josep M. Barnadas, "The Catholic Church in Colonial Spanish America," and Eduardo Hoonaert, "The Catholic Church in Colonial Brazil," in *Colonial Latin America*, vol. 1, *The Cambridge History of Latin America*, ed. Leslie Bethell (Cambridge: Cambridge University Press, 1984), 511–40 and 541–56. See also the now classic work, Tzvetan Todorov's *The Conquest of America: The Question of the Other* (New York: Harper & Row, 1984).

13. See Barth, *Church Dogmatics* IV/3.2, 797.

14. This is an expression of the fact that, strictly speaking, Christians do not possess wisdom. Christ being wisdom incarnate, it is the other way around. Properly understood, Christians are possessed by wisdom, and are wise not in themselves but just to the degree that wisdom dwells in them.

15. On the increasing commodification of everyday exchanges, see the essays in Susan Strasser, ed., *Commodifying Everything: Relationships of the Market* (London: Routledge, 2003).

16. On the importance of gift giving in human life, see Volf, *Free of Charge*, 55–126.

17. Though the apostle Paul thought that he had the right to be paid for his apostolic work, he forwent remuneration (see Acts 20:33–35; 1 Cor. 9:1–18; 2 Thess. 3:8). Socrates, as is well known, would not receive remuneration for his services (see Plato, *Apology* 19d–e).

18. See Volf, *Free of Charge*.

19. See Plato, *Theaetetus* 148e–150e.

20. See Søren Kierkegaard, *Philosophical Fragments*, trans. David F. Swenson and Howard V. Hong (Princeton: Princeton University Press, 1962), 11–45.

21. On "hearing" as fundamental to faith, see Ratzinger (Benedict XVI), *Introduction to Christianity*, 90–92.

22. For a literary exploration of this theme, see Paer Lagerkvist, *Barabbas*, trans. Alan Blair (New York: Vintage, 1989).

23. Sayyid Qutb, for instance, explicitly states that, while living in the West, he engaged in polemics with Christians, trying to show them the unreasonableness

of Christianity: "Look at these concepts of the Trinity, Original Sin, Sacrifice, and Redemption, which are agreeable neither to reason nor to conscience" (Qutb, *Milestones*, 95).

24. On the ability of disciples to perceive Christ, see a critical comment by Friedrich Nietzsche that presupposes the same conviction about the need for affinity between what is encountered and what is received (Nietzsche, *Twilight of the Idols and The Anti-Christ*,157). See also Volf, *Exclusion and Embrace*, 254–58.

25. So, for instance, Kierkegaard, *Philosophical Fragments*, 14–15.

26. See on this Werner W. Jaeger, *Early Christianity and Greek Paideia* (Cambridge, MA: Harvard University Press, 1961); and Jaroslav Pelikan, *Christianity and Classical Culture: The Metamorphosis of Natural Theology in the Christian Encounter with Hellenism* (New Haven: Yale University Press, 1993).

27. On the transformation of the adopted Greek philosophical vocabulary to suit the needs of the subject matter as understood by the Christian faith, see, among many others, John D. Zizioulas, "The Doctrine of the Holy Trinity: The Significance of the Cappadocian Contribution," in *Trinitarian Theology Today: Essays on Divine Being and Act*, ed. Christoph Schwöbel (Edinburgh: T&T Clark, 1995), 44–60.

28. On the phenomenon of give and take in the process of inculturation, see Chibueze Udeani, *Inculturation as Dialogue: Igbo Culture and the Message of Christ* (New York: Rodopi, 2007), 130–33.

29. Justin Martyr, *First Apology* 46.

30. Paul Tillich, *Systematic Theology* (Chicago: University of Chicago Press, 1963), 3:214.

31. With regard to Christians learning from Muslims, in *Allah* I write the following: "Each faith has a repertoire of beliefs and practices. At a given time or place, a faith will foreground some themes in its repertoire and background others. Currently, for instance, 'submission to God,' Islam's central theme, is not a favorite 'melody' of many Christians in the West; it runs counter to Western egalitarian cultural sensibilities. But it's an essential and oft 'performed' part of the historic Christian repertoire. After all, Christians believe that God is the sovereign Lord. It would be fully legitimate, and maybe even desirable, for Christians in the West, partly nudged by Muslims, to rediscover 'submission to God' as a key dimension of spirituality" (197).

32. For a brief discussion of some basic rules for evangelism based on the Golden Rule, see ibid., chap. 11.

33. Martin E. Marty's book *The Christian World: A Global History* (New York: Random House, 2007) includes numerous examples of Christians sharing wisdom in both good and bad ways.

34. This claim became popular following the publication of the Italian journalist Antonio Socci's book *The New Persecuted*, only available in the original Italian: *I Nuovo Perseguitati* (Casale Monferrato: Piemme, 2002). Socci derives many of his figures from David B. Barrett, George T. Kurian, and Todd M. Johnson, *The World Christian Encyclopedia*, 2 vols. (Oxford: Oxford University Press, 2001), which has been the subject of several criticisms. For an impartial assessment of the encyclopedia's data, see Becky Hsu et al., "Estimating the Religious Composition of

All Nations: An Empirical Assessment of the World Christian Database," *Journal for the Scientific Study of Religion* 47 (2008): 678–93.

35. See Robert Conquest, "The Churches and the People," in *The Harvest of Sorrow: Soviet Collectivization and the Terror-famine* (Oxford: Oxford University Press, 1986), 199–213; Geoffrey A. Hosking, "Religion and Nationality under the Soviet State," in *The First Socialist Society: A History of the Soviet Union from Within*, rev. ed. (Cambridge, MA: Harvard University Press, 1993), 227–60; Richard C. Bush Jr., *Religion in Communist China* (Nashville: Abingdon, 1970); G. Thompson Brown, *Christianity in the People's Republic of China*, rev. ed. (Atlanta: John Knox, 1986), 75–134.

36. On forgiveness, see Volf, *Free of Charge*, chaps. 4–6.

37. See John Paul II, "Jubilee Characteristic: The Purification of Memory," *Origins* 29 (2000): 649–50.

38. Martin Luther, *Works*, ed. Harold J. Grimm (Philadelphia: Fortress, 1962), 31:306.

Chapter 7 Public Engagement

1. This phrase originated with Friedrich Engels, who used it to describe what happens to the state in the aftermath of the proletarian revolution. "The state is not 'abolished.' *It withers away*" (*Anti-Dühring: Herr Eugen Dühring's Revolution in Science*, 2nd ed. [Moscow: Foreign Languages Publishing, 1954], 387, my italics).

2. See, for example, Ernest Renan, *The Future of Science* (Boston: Roberts Brothers, 1891); and Jean-Marie Gayau, *The Non-Religion of the Future: A Sociological Study* (New York: Holt, 1897).

3. See Karl Marx, "A Contribution to the Critique of Hegel's *Philosophy of Right*: Introduction," and "Concerning Feuerbach," in *Karl Marx: Early Writings*, trans. Rodney Livingstone and Gregor Benton (London: Penguin, 1992), 243–58 and 421–23; Friedrich Nietzsche, *On the Genealogy of Morality*, ed. Keith Ansell-Pearson, trans. Carol Diethe (Cambridge: Cambridge University Press, 1994); Sigmund Freud, *The Future of an Illusion*, trans. James Strachey (1961; repr., New York: W. W. Norton, 1989).

4. See Peter Berger, "The Desecularization of the World: A Global Overview," in *The Desecularization of the World: Resurgent Religion and World Politics*, ed. Peter Berger (Grand Rapids: Eerdmans, 1999), 1–18.

5. See Shmuel N. Eisenstadt, "The Transformation of the Religious Dimension in the Constitution of Contemporary Modernities—The Contemporary Religious Sphere in the Context of Multiple Modernities," in *Religion in Cultural Discourse: Essays in Honor of Hans J. Kippenberg on the Occasion of His 65th Birthday*, ed. Brigitte Luchesi and Kocku von Stuckrad (New York: Walter de Gruyter, 2004), 337–53.

6. Charles Taylor, *Modern Social Imaginaries* (Durham: Duke University Press, 2004), 1; Charles Taylor, "Two Theories of Modernity," in *Alternative Modernities*, ed. Dilip Parmeshwar Gaonkar (Durham: Duke University Press, 2001), 172–96. On multiple modernities, see also Jose Casanova, "Rethinking Secularization: A Global Comparative Perspective," in *Religion, Globalization, and Culture*, ed. Peter Beyer and Lori Beaman (Leiden: Brill, 2007), 107–10.

7. I'm somewhat hesitant to designate any of the world's faiths as "religions" because the very notion of "religion" is a product of modernity; it represents the reduction of a living and encompassing faith to a sphere—a religious one—within the larger secular society (see, among others, Cavanaugh, *Myth of Religious Violence*, 57–122).

8. See Philip Jenkins, *The Next Christendom: The Coming of Global Christianity* (Oxford: Oxford University Press, 2002), 42–46.

9. See "U.S. Religious Landscape Survey—Religious Affiliation: Diverse and Dynamic," Pew Forum on Religion and Public Life, February 2008, available at http://religions.pewforum.org/pdf/report-religious-landscape-study-full.pdf; "Mapping the Global Muslim Population," Pew Forum on Religion and Public Life, October 2009, available at http://pewforum.org/uploadedfiles/Topics/Demographics/Muslimpopulation.pdf. With the exception of the Muslim estimate, for which Pew provides an absolute figure, I have come to these figures by multiplying the Pew data regarding population percentages by the U.S. Census Bureau's estimate for the U.S. population in 2009. The "nonreligious" figure includes those whom the Pew Forum counts as "atheist," "agnostic," and "secular unaffiliated." On the difficulty of estimating the size of Muslim populations in Europe and the United States, see Jocelyn Cesari, *When Islam and Democracy Meet: Muslims in Europe and the United States* (New York: Palgrave Macmillan, 2004), 9–11.

10. See Robert J. Pauly Jr., *Islam in Europe: Integration or Marginalization?* (Aldershot: Ashgate, 2004), which includes examples of Muslim communities becoming more involved in local and national electoral politics in a number of European countries.

11. See a recent report about companies in China actively fostering Christian religious activity among their workers: Christopher Landau, "Christian Faith Plus Chinese Productivity," BBC News, August 26, 2010, http://www.bbc.co.uk/news/world-asia-pacific-10942954.

12. On the plurality of religions in India, see T. N. Madan, "Religions of India: Plurality and Pluralism," in *Religious Pluralism in South Asia and Europe*, ed. Jamal Malik and Helmut Reifeld (Oxford: Oxford University Press, 2005), 42–76; Kamran Ahmad, *Roots of Religious Tolerance in Pakistan and India* (Lahore: Vanguard, 2008).

13. For an example of this sort of language, see the remarks of Giacomo Cardinal Biffi quoted in Cesari, *When Islam and Democracy Meet*:

It is obvious that Muslims must be treated as a separate case. We must have faith that those who are responsible for the public good will not fear to confront it with eyes open and without illusions. In the vast majority of cases, and with only a few exceptions, Muslims come here with the resolve to remain strangers to our brand of individual or social "humanity" in everything that is most essential, most precious: strangers to what it is impossible for us to give up as "secularists." More or less openly, they come here with their minds made up to remain fundamentally "different," waiting to make us all become fundamentally like them. . . . I believe that Europe must either become Christian again, or else it will become Muslim. (33)

14. See Richard T. Hughes, *Christian America and the Kingdom of God* (Champaign: University of Illinois Press, 2009), chaps. 4–5.

Notes

15. See Wolterstorff, "Role of Religion," 67–120; cf. John Rawls, *Political Liberalism* (New York: Columbia University Press, 1993).

16. Wolterstorff, "Role of Religion," 73.

17. For this phrase, see Thomas Jefferson, "To Messrs. Nehemiah Dodge, Ephram Robbins, and Stephen S. Nelson, a Committee of the Danbury Baptist Association, in the State of Connecticut," in *Thomas Jefferson: Political Writings*, ed. Joyce Appleby and Terence Ball (Cambridge: Cambridge University Press, 1999), 397.

18. As an example of the critique of political liberalism along the lines I have noted above, consider the position of Oliver O'Donovan. In a paper entitled "The Constitutional State and Limitation of Belief" delivered at Yale on March 23, 2006 (available at http://www.yale.edu/divinity/video/theocracy/first.shtml), he raises the issue of the character of the relationship between what he calls the "terms of civic association" in a given polity (understood as regulative principles) and "universal visions" (the comprehensive theoretical doctrines of its inhabitants). The regulative principles are "second-order" claims; "universal visions" are first-order claims. In liberal democracies second-order rules regulate the public expression of first-order universal visions. As a consequence, such democracies are inhospitable to believers, who must subordinate their comprehensive, action-guiding visions to the rules of civic association. Religious citizens of these democracies experience, therefore, "a radical incoherence" in the structure of their belief systems. That is a very serious charge. If correct, liberal democracies are failing to satisfy one of political liberalism's own most basic stated goals: to ensure freedom for each person to live in accordance with his or her own interpretation of life (or lack of it). Liberalism is illiberal. Incoherence in the structure of belief systems (universal vision) for members of liberal democracies translates to incoherence in the project of political liberalism itself. To live in a liberal democracy, believers must engage in "bad compromises" by giving in, against their "deepest convictions," to an outside set of regulations—in other words, to alter instead of exercise their universal visions. Just for these reasons and others, O'Donovan rejects political liberalism. Along with Wolterstorff, I think that political liberalism can be "fixed."

19. Wolterstorff, "Role of Religion," 115.

20. Ibid.

21. Ibid., 109.

22. Ibid.

23. See Volf, *Allah*, chap. 12. See also Volf, *Captive to the Word of God*, chap. 3.

24. Jalal al-Din Rumi, *Masnavi* 3.1259, quoted, for instance, in Geoffrey Parrinder, *The Routledge Dictionary of Religious and Spiritual Citations* (London: Routledge, 2000), 22.

25. For a classic presentation of the view, see John Hick, *An Interpretation of Religion: Human Responses to the Transcendent* (New Haven: Yale University Press, 1989).

26. For a critique of the pluralist account of religion, see Gavin D'Costa, *The Meeting of Religions and the Trinity* (Maryknoll, NY: Orbis, 2000); Michael Barnes, *Theology and the Dialogue of Religions* (Cambridge: Cambridge University Press, 2002).

27. See William Schweiker on religions finding themselves in what he describes as a situation of "reflectivity"—each seeing itself also from the perspective of the other and readjusting its own self-understanding partly in response—in *Theological Ethics and Global Dynamics: In the Time of Many Worlds* (Oxford: Blackwell, 2004).

28. See Volf, *Allah*, chap. 1.

29. For an analogous account of the relation between the Christian faith and culture more broadly construed, see chap. 5.

30. See John Richard Bowen, *Why the French Don't Like Headscarves: Islam, the State, and Public Space* (Princeton: Princeton University Press, 2007), for a discussion of perhaps the most publicized confrontation between a strident secularism and Islam.

31. To do just this was the genius of the Muslim initiative called "A Common Word." For the document, one response, and theological analysis of central issues, see *A Common Word: Muslims and Christians on Loving God and Neighbor*, ed. Miroslav Volf, Ghazi bin Muhammad, and Melissa Yarrington (Grand Rapids: Eerdmans, 2010).

32. See Volf, *Captive to the Word of God*, 109.

33. See chapter 5. See also Volf, "The Trinity Is Our Social Program."

34. Gotthold Ephraim Lessing, *Nathan the Wise*, trans. Ronald Schechter (Boston: Bedford/St. Martin's, 2004), 56.

35. Ibid., 76.

36. Ibid., 57.

37. See on this the movement called "Scriptural Reasoning": *The Promise of Scriptural Reasoning*, ed. David Ford and C. C. Pecknold (Oxford: Blackwell, 2006). Cf. Volf, *Captive to the Word of God*, 38–39.

38. For the importance of robust public debate, see Amy Gutmann and Dennis Frank Thompson, *Democracy and Disagreement* (Cambridge, MA: Harvard University Press, 1996). See also the critiques of Gutmann and Thompson from a number of perspectives in *Deliberative Politics: Essays on Democracy and Disagreement*, ed. Stephen Macedo (Oxford: Oxford University Press, 1999).

39. What William James observed about religious belief is also true, I think, of political decisions. "Indeed we *may* wait if we will . . . but if we do so, we do so at our peril as much as if we believed. In either case we *act*, taking our life in our hands" ("The Will to Believe," in *The Writings of William James: A Comprehensive Edition*, ed. John J. McDermott [New York: Random House, 1967], 734). James closes his essay with the following quotation from James Fitzjames Stephen:

> Each must act as he thinks best; and if he is wrong, so much the worse for him. We stand on a mountain pass in the midst of whirling snow and blinding mist, through which we get glimpses now and then of paths which may be deceptive. If we stand still we shall be frozen to death. If we take the wrong road we shall be dashed to pieces. We do not certainly know whether there is any right one. What must we do? "Be strong and of a good courage." Act for the best, hope for the best, and take what comes. (*Liberty, Equality, Fraternity* [New York: Holt & Williams, 1873], 333)

Conclusion

1. The full text of the speech, including all the material quoted in this chapter, can be found at http://www.nytimes.com/2009/06/04/us/politics/04obama.text .html.

2. This particular formulation of the "Golden Rule" is specifically Christian. It positively mandates doing unto others as we want done unto us. Islam has a similar positive version of the rule: "None of you has faith until you love for your neighbor what you love for yourself" (so Muhammad according to *Sahih Muslim, Kitab al-Iman* 72). Some other religions formulate the rule negatively: don't do unto others what you don't want them to do unto you (see, e.g., Confucius, *Analects* 15.24).

3. Samuel P. Huntington, *The Clash of Civilizations and the Remaking of World Order* (New York: Simon & Schuster, 1996).

4. See "Mapping the Global Muslim Population," Pew Forum on Religion and Public Life, October 7, 2009, http://pewforum.org/Mapping-the-Global-Muslim -Population.aspx. (But recall the difficulty of arriving at an accurate estimate.)

5. For Islam, see Abdullahi Ahmed An-Na'im, *Islam and the Secular State: Negotiating the Future of Shari'a* (Cambridge, MA: Harvard University Press, 2008); Feisal Abdul Rauf, *What's Right with Islam: A New Vision for Muslims and the West* (New York: HarperCollins, 2004).

6. Qutb, *Milestones*, 2.

7. Ibid., 89.

8. Eboo Patel, *Acts of Faith: The Story of an American Muslim, the Struggle for the Soul of a Generation* (Boston: Beacon, 2008).

Index

Abdul Quddus of Gangoh, 6
abortion issue, 4–5
Abrahamic faiths. *See* monotheism
absolute hospitality, 46–47
accommodation, 84–85, 94–96
active faith. *See* work
adventus, 56
Alchemy of Happiness, The (al-Ghazali),
  63–64, 66
Ambivalence of the Sacred, The
  (Appleby), 51
American dreams, 60–61, 99–100
Anti-Christ, The (Nietzsche), 4
Appleby, R. Scott, 51
ascent, 7, 8–9, 73, 104–5. *See also* return
  functional reduction of, 9–11
  idolatric substitution of, 12–13
Augustine
  on human flourishing, 58, 70–72
  on restless hearts, 151n9
authority. *See* wisdom

Balkan Wars of the 1990s, 39, 53,
  155n29
Barth, Karl, 106–7, 151n11
blessing, 16, 24–27
Bloom, Paul, 160n30
Bonhoeffer, Dietrich, 87–88

boundaries, 81, 96, 132–33
*Bridge Betrayed: Religion and Genocide
  in Bosnia, The* (Sells), 155n29
Buddhism, 8, 122
Bush, George W., 140, 160n4

Cairo Speech (Obama), 139–41
capitalism, 14
Caputo, John, 46
Carey, William, 105
Carroll, Lewis, 33
Casanova, José, 158n5
center of faith, the, 130–33, 166n31
Certeau, Michel de, 89–90
Chesterton, G. K., 84
Christ and Culture (Niebuhr), xiv–xv
Christianity, xvii. *See also* new Christian
  identity
  active faith in, 151n11
  bearing witness in, xvi
  cross-cultural missionary work of, 105
  dominion theology in, xi
  early communities in, 78–79
  functions of faith in, 16, 132
  Golden Rule of, xvi–xvii, 114, 126,
    140–45, 154n14, 167n2
  growth of, 120–22, 164n9, 164n13
  healing of nations in, 3–4

living well in, xvii
on love, 72–74
malfunctions in, 4–6
monotheism of, 41–43, 154n14
Niebuhr on relation with culture of,
xiv–xv
as one of many players, 77–97, 132–33
as prophetic religion, xv, 4, 7–8, 78
on religious pluralism, 141–45
thin and thick faith in, 39–41, 43–44,
48, 50–51, 153n6, 154n8
totalitarian forms of, 150n12
violent character of, 39–43, 51–54,
154n8
vocabulary of, 91–92
as way of life, 101, 142–44, 160n4
Christian Right, 78
churches (vs. sects), 80–84, 158n5
City of God (Augustine), 58
clash of civilizations, 139–41
coercive faith, xv–xvi, 12–13, 17–21,
37–54, 73, 144–45. See also violence
in accounts of creation, 43–46
in accounts of redemption, 46–48
in the book of Revelation, 48
irrelevant faith in, 19, 20
monotheist assertions in, 41–43,
154n14
thinned out faith in, 19–20, 39–41,
43–44, 48, 50–51, 153n6, 154n8
unwillingness to walk the narrow path
in, 19, 20–21
common good, the, xvi, 4–5, 78. See
also human flourishing
common principles, 139–41. See also
Golden Rule
"Common Word, A," 166n31
community, 33–34
compassion, 71
conflict, 100, 116–17, 161n12
conformation, 85–87
conquest and colonization, 90
consocial engagement, 125–30, 166n27
Constantine I, Emperor of Rome, 48
Cosmic Reason, 67
Cosmopolis: The Hidden Agenda of
Modernity (Toulmin), 152n3
creation, 43–46
creativity, 8–9, 24
culture, xiv–xvii, 89–97
Curse of Cain: The Violent Legacy of
Monotheism, The (Schwartz), 41

Delbanco, Andrew, 60–61, 62, 99, 156n10
deliverance, 16, 27–29
Derrida, Jacques, 46
difference. See internal differentiation
discernment, 30–31
Discipleship (Bonhoeffer), 87–88
dissatisfaction, 61–62, 99–100, 156n15,
156n16
diversity, 121–23, 128–29, 164n13
dominion theology, xi
Durkheim, Emile, 38

Eagleton, Terry, 69
early Christian communities, 78–79
Education's End (Kronman), 65–66,
157n34
Eisenstadt, Shmuel, 120
elimination of religion, 38–39, 152n3.
See also secularism
End of Faith, The (Harris), 18
engaged faith, 96–97. See also religious
political pluralism
public engagement in, 119–37
sharing of wisdom in, 99–117
Engels, Friedrich, 163n1
Ethics of Memory, The (Margalit),
153n6

failure and deliverance, 24–27
faith, 16, 130–33, 166n31. See also
specific faiths, e.g., Christianity
active faith (see work)
coercive faith (see coercive faith)
engaged faith (see engaged faith)
idleness of (see idleness of faith)
malfunctioning of (see malfunctioning
faith)
prophetic faith (see prophetic faith)
thick faith (see thick faith)
thin faith (see thin faith)
Feuerbach, Ludwig, 5
fit with reality, 66–69, 71
forgiveness and repentance, 114–16
Freud, Sigmund, 5
functional reduction of faith, 10–11, 73
futurum, 56

Gay Science, The (Nietzsche), 10–11
Geertz, Clifford, 153n6
generosity, 133–36
al-Ghazali, Abu Hamid Muhammad,
63–65, 66

Index

giving of wisdom, 106–13. *See also*
    wisdom
Golden Rule, xvi–xvii, 114, 126, 140–45,
    154n14, 167n2
Grand Study of Harvard University,
    156n16
great commandment, 104
Greek philosophical tradition, 111–12,
    162n27
Grünewald, Matthias, 107
guidance toward moral activity, 30–32
Guide of the Perplexed, The
    (Maimonides), 64, 66, 157n22

Harris, Sam, 18
Hauerwas, Stanley, 85
healing of nations, 3–4
Hebrew Bible, 111
Hegel, Georg W. F., 92
hermeneutical hospitality, 136–37,
    166n39
higher humans (Nietzsche), 67–68,
    157n31
Hinduism, 122
hope
    in human flourishing, 55–56, 60–61,
        156n10
    in sharing of wisdom, 116–17
Hope and History (Pieper), 55
Hsu, Becky, et al., 162n34
human flourishing, 55–74. *See also*
    love's role in human flourishing
Augustine's view of, 70–72
centrality in faith of, 63–66, 157n22
Christian scriptures on, 72–74
compassion in, 71
fit with reality of, 66–69, 71
hope in, 55–56, 60–61, 156n10
meaningfulness of life in, 65–66
role of community in, 33–34
satisfaction and pleasure in, 57–62,
    68–69, 72, 156nn15–16, 160n30
universal solidarity in, 58–60
humanism, 59, 65–66, 120, 157n34
Huntington, Samuel, 140–41

identity. *See* new Christian identity
idleness of faith, 12–21
    active faith in response to, 24–36
    misdirected busyness in, 29–30
    power of systems in, 13–15, 19, 20
    temptation in, 12–13, 19, 20–21, 73

idolatric substitution, 12–13, 73
imposition of faith. *See* coercive faith
inculturation, 96–97. *See also* new
    Christian identity
internal differentiation, 89–93
    accommodation *vs.*, 94–96
    engagement with the world in, 96–97
    total cultural transformation *vs.*,
        93–94
internet, the, 83
Interpretation of Cultures (Geertz),
    153n6
Iqbal, Muhammad, 6–7
irrelevant faith, 19, 20
"Is Maimonides's Ideal Person Austerely
    Rationalist?" (Kellner), 157n22
Islam, 6–7, 122
    Christian critiques of, 157n23
    "A Common Word" initiative, 166n31
    Golden Rule of, 167n2
    growth of, 120–21, 141, 164n9,
        164n13
    moral universe of, 151n19
    Obama's statements on, 139–41
    Qutb's totalitarian view of, x–xiv, 88,
        141–44, 149n10, 160n4, 161n23
    as way of life, 142–44, 160n4
    wisdom in, 162n31

James, William, 167n2
Jesus Christ
    ascent and return of, 7
    death of, 48
    as wisdom incarnate, 106–9, 161n14
John Paul II, Pope, 115
John's Gospel, 111–12
John the Baptist, 107
Judaism, 7, 111, 121–22, 145
Jurgensmeyer, Mark, 38, 154n8
Justin Martyr, 112
just war theory, 30

Kant, Immanuel, 28
Kellner, Menachem, 157n22
Kronman, Anthony, 65–66, 157n34
Kruhonja, Katarina, 52

Lessing, Gotthold Ephraim, 133–36
liberal democracy, 123–30, 137, 165n18
Licklider, J. C. R., 83
Lilla, Mark, x
Lincoln, Abraham, 60

171

postliberal approaches, 85–87, 159n23
poststructuralism, 46–47
power, 26–27
power of systems, 13–14, 19, 20
prayer, 25
prophetic faith, xv, 4
    the common good in, xvi, 4–5, 78
    creative return in, 7, 8–9, 12–21, 73
    receptive ascent in, 7, 8–12, 73
    sharing of wisdom in, 104–5
    transformational nature of, 6–8
    as way of life, 101, 142–44, 160n4
*Protestant Ethic and the Spirit of
    Capitalism, The* (Weber), 14
Protestant missionary movement, 105
public engagement, 119–37. *See also*
    engaged faith
    consocial proposal for, 125–30, 166n27
    growth of religion in, 120–21
    in liberal democracy, 123–25, 165n18
    religious diversity in, 121–23, 128–29,
        164n13

Qutb, Sayyid, x–xiv, 88, 141–44, 149n10,
    160n4, 161n23

rationality, 154n8
Real American Dream, The (Delbanco),
    60–61, 99
receiving of wisdom, 8–9, 109–13,
    161n14, 161n17, 162n27, 162n31
*Reconstruction of Religious Thought in
    Islam, The* (Iqbal), 6–7
redemption, 46–48
reflectivity, 166n27
*Religion, the Missing Dimension
    of Statecraft* (ed. Johnston and
    Sampson), 37
religious diversity, 121–23, 128–29,
    164n13
religious persecution, 105, 114, 161n9,
    162n34
religious political pluralism, xi, xiv–xvii,
    141–45
    consocial proposal for, 125–30, 166n27
    generosity in, 133–36
    hermeneutical hospitality in, 136–37,
        167n39
    in new Christian identity, 81–82,
        132–33, 154n14, 158n5
    in Obama's Cairo Speech, 139–41
    reduction of particularity in, 127–30

religious diversity in, 121–23, 128–29,
    164n13
    speaking from the center of faith in,
        130–33, 166n31
repentance, 114–16
return, 12–21, 73, 105. *See also* ascent
    coercive faith in, xv–xvi, 12–13, 17–21
    idleness of faith in, 12–17, 18
reverse prophetism, 113
Rieff, Philip, 57–58
Right of Livelihood Award, 53
"Role of Religion in Decision and
    Discussion of Political Issues, The"
    (Wolterstorff), 124–27
Rorty, Richard, 156n10
Ruether, Rosemary Radford, 44
Ryle, Gilbert, 153n6

satisfaction (pleasure), 57–62, 68–69, 72,
    145, 156nn15–16, 160n30
Schopenhauer, Arthur, 156n15
Schwartz, Regina, 41, 42
Schweiker, William, 166n27
sects (*vs.* churches), 80–84, 158n5
Secular Age, A (Taylor), 59
secularism, x, 124–25, 131–32
    decline of religion in, 10–11, 38–39,
        73, 119–20, 152n3, 163n1
    humanism of, 59, 65–66, 120, 156n10,
        157n34
self, the, 60–61
    as giver of wisdom, 106–9, 161n14
    as receiver of wisdom, 111–13
Sells, Michael, 155n29
Seneca, 66–67
separation of church and state, 124–25
separatism, 85–87, 159n23
September 11, 2001, attacks, 37, 38–39,
    54
Sexism and God-Talk (Ruether), 44
Shakespeare, William, 62
sharing wisdom. *See* wisdom
sins of commission, 13
sins of omission, 13
Socci, Antonio, 162n34
Socrates, 108, 161n17
Stoicism, 66–67, 71

Taylor, Charles, 59, 74, 120
temptation and integrity, 13, 19, 20–21
Terror in the Mind of God
    (Jurgensmeyer), 38, 154n8